IMAGES
of America

AFRICAN AMERICANS
IN HAWAI'I

IMAGES
of America

AFRICAN AMERICANS
IN HAWAI'I

D. Molentia Guttman and Ernest Golden
African American Diversity
Cultural Center Hawai'i

ARCADIA
PUBLISHING

Copyright © 2011 by D. Molentia Guttman and Ernest Golden, African American Diversity
Cultural Center Hawai'i
ISBN 978-0-7385-8116-3

Published by Arcadia Publishing
Charleston, South Carolina

Printed in the United States of America

Library of Congress Control Number: 2010924214

For all general information, please contact Arcadia Publishing:
Telephone 843-853-2070
Fax 843-853-0044
E-mail sales@arcadiapublishing.com
For customer service and orders:
Toll-Free 1-888-313-2665

Visit us on the Internet at www.arcadiapublishing.com

*To Barack Obama, who is the first African American
president and was born and raised in Hawai'i.*

*The people of African descent, past and present 'ohana (families), have
given much to the history of the Hawaiian Islands since the late 1700s.*

CONTENTS

ACKNOWLEDGMENTS

We are deeply grateful to Prof. Kathryn Waddell Takara for her tireless work in uncovering in local archives much of the history of blacks in Hawai'i, including her research data for her postdoctoral thesis at the University of Hawai'i. A special mahalo (thanks) to Stanley Ali for discovering the work of Alice A. Ball, who was instrumental in finding a cure for Hansen's disease (leprosy) from the oil found in chaulmoogra seeds in the chemistry laboratory at the University of Hawai'i in 1914. Many thanks to Miles Jackson, for publishing two books about African Americans in Hawai'i; Lorraine D. Henderson, for focusing her doctoral thesis about blacks in Hawai'i; Ray Emory, for sharing his research on the predominantly African American 29th Chemical Decontamination Company West Loch Tragedy; Deanna Paiva-Swinford, for sharing the history of the Paiva family who came to Hawai'i in 1883; and numerous scholars at the University of Hawai'i who have written articles about the history of people of African descent in the Hawaiian Islands.

Without the support of Evangeline, the wife of Ernest Golden, and Steven, the husband of D. Molentia Guttman, this book could not have materialized. They deserve a special mahalo nui loa (thank-you). We thank the local African American church pastors and the sorority and fraternal organizations in Hawai'i for their collaboration. We also appreciate and thank the researchers and archivists at Bishop Museum, University of Hawai'i Hamilton Library Archives, Hawai'i State Archives, Hawaiian Children's Society, and Mission House Museum. Many thanks to the late Bob Krauss, editor of the *Honolulu Advertiser*, for sharing his experiences about African American celebrities who entertained at nightclubs in downtown Honolulu in the 1940s and 1950s. He also shared journalistic documentation of people of African descent dating back to the early 1900s. A special mahalo to Debbie Seracini, editor at Arcadia Publishing.

Images used throughout this book came from the following sources: Bishop Museum Archives, University of Hawai'i Hamilton Library Archives, Moorland-Spingarn Research Center, Elizabeth Schlesinger Library on the History of Women, *Hawaiian Journal of History*, Montana Historical Society, *Can Anything Beat White?* by Elisabeth Petry, Deanne Paiva-Swinford, Ernest Golden, D. Molentia Guttman, The Links, Alpha Kappa Alpha Sorority, Honolulu Black Nurses, Honolulu NAACP, National Military Archives, *Honolulu Magazine*, *Ebony* magazine, Kathryn W. Takara, Don Brown, Ernestine Jennings, Dolores D. Reece, *Nolle Smith: Cowboy, Engineer, Statesman* by Bobette Gugliotta, *And They Came* and *They Followed the Trade Winds* by Miles Jackson, *Why Me?* by Alonzo DeMello, *Mahogany* magazine, *Honolulu Advertiser*, *Honolulu Star-Bulletin*, authors D. Molentia Guttman (DG) and Ernest Golden (EG), and many other private sources.

INTRODUCTION

When the first black men arrived in the Hawaiian Islands in the late 1700s, they were greeted by the native Hawaiians who lived in grass huts scattered sparsely throughout the lush valleys and along the shoreline. During the late 1700s and early 1800s, many people of African ancestry came to Hawaii aboard merchant and whaling ships. These individuals brought with them skills including masonry, barbering, carpentry, stewarding, and tailoring. Acting as administrators and interpreters for the monarchy, some served as advisors to King Kamehameha I, who welcomed black men from around the world to the Hawaiian Islands. Others became entrepreneurs, musicians, and small businessmen serving foreigners. Nantucket Quaker seamen also made the whaling industry a thriving business. At a time when Africans were still being sold into slavery, Yankee whalers signed on African Portuguese from the Cape Verde Islands off the coast of Africa, blacks from the Caribbean, and black Americans as seamen, whose service took them across the face of the earth, across the Pacific, and into the Hawaiian Islands. Since the 1770s, the islands have been home to people of African descent, who have made tremendous contributions to Hawai'i for over two centuries.

The most notable among early African Americans arriving in the Hawaiian Island was Anthony D. Allen from Schenectady, New York. He was 24 years old and probably a slave when he left Boston on a merchant ship that took him to China, the Caribbean, the Pacific Northwest, and finally to Hawai'i.

The first black woman to arrive in the Hawaiian Islands was Betsey Stockton in 1823. She was 18 when she sailed with the Stewart family from New Haven, Connecticut, on the ship *Thames*. Betsey was given her freedom by Rev. Dr. Ashbel Green in Princeton, New Jersey, after 1818. Educated under his tutelage, she learned to read and write and later studied mathematics and science. Rev. Charles Samuel Stewart was a close friend of the Green family. He had been selected from the missionary board to go to Hawai'i with the second group of missionaries to arrive in the islands. Before his departure, he married and needed a housekeeper for his wife. He asked Reverend Green if Betsey could accompany them with the missionary board's approval. The missionary board stipulated that Betsey not be used as a domestic in any other missionary household except the Stewarts' and that she perform her duties as a missionary teacher. Betsey learned to speak the Hawaiian language and had a great relationship with the Native Hawaiian people. She taught Hawaiian women how to sew Western fashions and introduced Western-style children care and housekeeping skills. The Hawaiian chiefs (royal families) were taught to read and write by the missionaries. Later, Betsey began a school for commoners (maka'ainana) to teach them how to read and write. In 1824, a school for the commoner was established, and Betsey was its first superintendent. This was the first public school in Hawai'i.

For over a century, people of African descent followed the underground voyage to freedom on the high seas to the Hawaiian Islands. These black pioneers included a young man in his late teens who came to Hawai'i as a defense worker, along with approximately 400 to 500 other young men and women hired by the Department of the Navy and the Department of War, after the bombing of Pearl Harbor on December 7, 1941. Hundreds of black enlisted men were already serving on ships as mess hall attendants and domestics. On shore, at military bases, they served as stevedores and road builders or worked in other forms of manual labor. Despite the extenuating conditions of discrimination and segregation, black infantrymen and sailors met the challenge, persevered, and served with distinction and honor, although they were seldom recognized for their services.

In Hawai'i, the contributions of African Americans to the naval base at Pearl Harbor, other military installations, and the community are enormous. This revealing history has been kept silent, as if in a corner of America's closet.

One

PIONEERS OF AFRICAN DESCENT IN THE HAWAIIAN KINGDOM

Anthony D. Allen left Boston when he was hired as a seaman. His sea journeys took him around the world, with adventures including pirate attacks, incarceration, and a shipwreck. People he met during his eight years of travels included Toussaint L'Overture, liberator of Haiti, and the famous British admiral Lord Nelson. On his last trip from China to America, his ship stopped in Hawai'i, which he had previously visited. Allen decided that it was time to leave the sea and settled in Honolulu in 1810. (Courtesy *Honolulu Magazine*.)

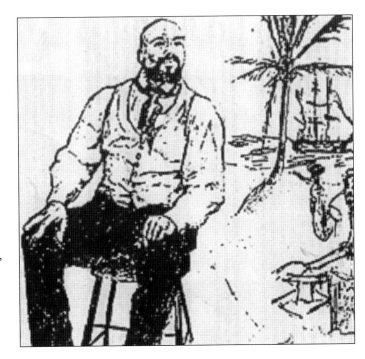

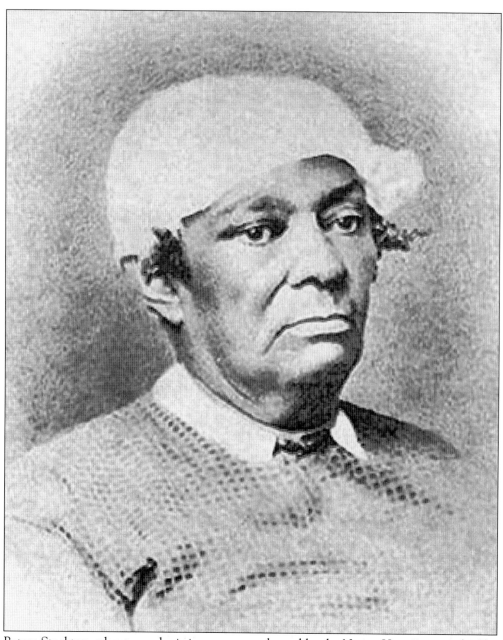

Betsey Stockton, educator and missionary, was embraced by the Native Hawaiian people. She was seen walking around the community dressed in white and wearing a matching proffered African-style head wrap. Betsey's gathering place was under a big banyan tree in the Lahainaluna neighborhood surrounded by Hawaiian women and children. She taught the Hawaiian women Western skills in taking care of their children to keep them from getting sick but used Hawaiian herbs to heal children's sores and skin rashes. She also taught them Western housekeeping skills to keep the grass huts sanitary. An elegantly dignified 18-year-old Betsey Stockton was the first African American woman to embark on the shores of the Hawaiian Islands. She learned to speak the Hawaiian language fluently and founded the Lahainaluna School for maka'ainana (commoners) on Maui in 1824. (Courtesy *Hawaiian Journal of History*.)

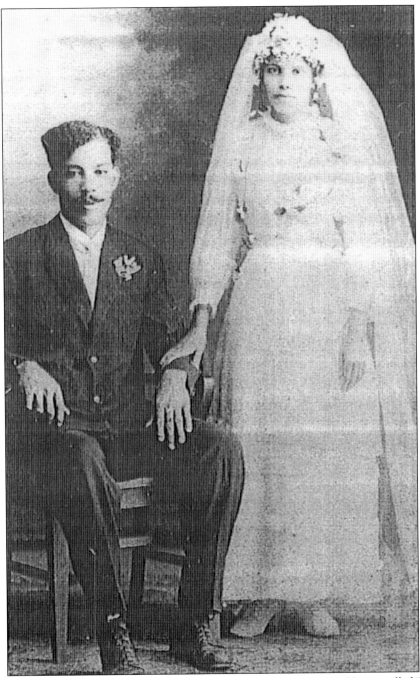

Frank Paiva Jr. was born in Kaupa'a on Hawai'i (Big Island) on May 26, 1892. He was called "Tupert," derived from *preto*, the Portuguese word for black. His father, Frank Paiva Sr., was born in Parana, Brazil, in 1861. When Frank Sr. was old enough, he was hired as a seaman on a commercial ship sailing the high seas. He jumped ship in Hilo and made the Big Island his home. He met Frank Jr.'s mother, Shendrina Alice, who came to Hawai'i from Portugal. Frank Jr. married Mary daSilva in Papaikou, Hawai'i, as seen here on their wedding day. They had four children—Manual, Annie, Florence, and Albert. Their descendants still live in the islands. (Courtesy D. P. Swinford.)

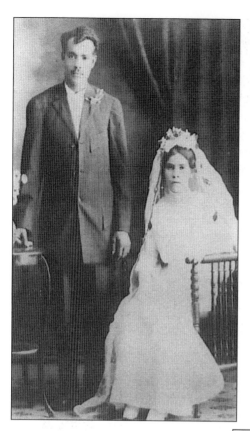

Charles Valencia Paiva was the second son of Frank Paiva Sr. Shown here on their wedding day, Charles married Mary Ables, and they had 13 children. His great-grandfather Franca (Francisco Franca) married Alexandrina Pavao in Hilo on October 15, 1888. (Courtesy D. P. Swinford.)

Pedro "Peter" Jose was born in Honolulu in 1881. His father came from the Cape Verde Islands off the coast of Africa. Cape Verdeans were of African Portuguese ancestry. Jose was a Honolulu policeman who had a great personality. He was well known in the downtown Honolulu area, near Aloha Tower, as the Hula Cop because he danced the hula while conducting street traffic. (Courtesy Bishop Museum.)

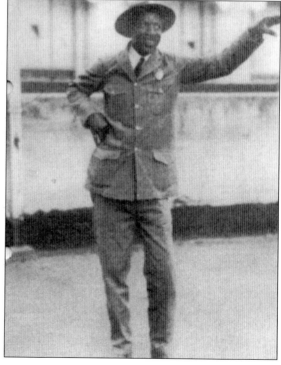

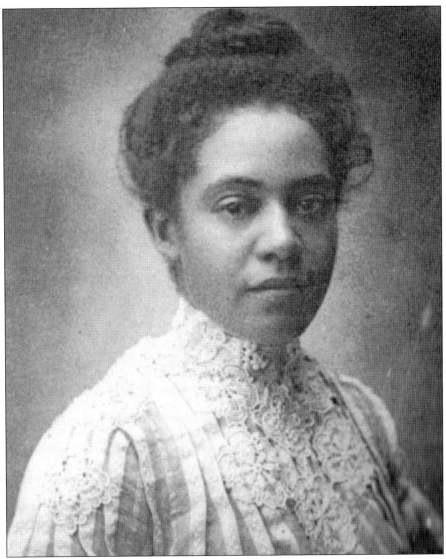

Helen James was a student from the Hampton Institute—founded by Samuel Chapman Armstrong, who was born and raised in Hawai'i—who came to the islands to teach in 1901. She was chaperoned by Charles and Estrelle Dykes. Charles was the new principal of the Kamehameha Schools, founded for the benefit of children of Hawaiian descent. Helen was assigned kitchen and parlor duties. Despite the long hours, Helen took on additional duties tutoring a student in English and assisting the school nurse and preparing her lectures. There were two students under surveillance for leprosy. In addition, the nursing staff was treating students with measles and other minor ailments. One student suffered terrible pain from a school accident. He had been given morphine for six weeks to relieve his pain. Despite her busy schedule, she found ample time for socializing. One day, Queen Lili'uokalani came to Kamehameha School accompanied by her ward Joseph Iia, who was a candidate for West Point. Helen was honored to meet and shake the queen's hand. On another occasion, Helen was introduced to Thomas McCants Stewart and his wife, Alice, who called on Charles and Estrella Dykes. She had the opportunity to observe other black people in her travels around town and was surprised to see so many of them in Honolulu. (Courtesy Elizabeth Schlesinger Library on the History of Women.)

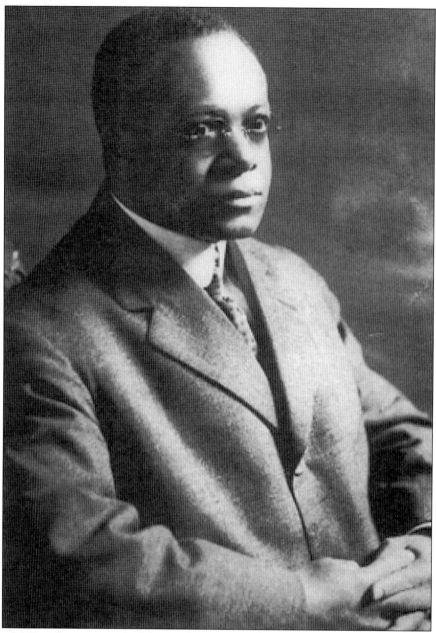

Thomas McCant Stewart came with his family to Hawai'i in 1898, five years after Queen Lili'uokalani was overthrown and the same year the Hawaiian Kingdom was annexed. He was a prominent civil rights attorney in New York who became immersed in local politics and took up the causes of the Hawaiian people, defending their land rights, and the Chinese who were denied rights under the Chinese Exclusionary Act. His contributions to Hawai'i included drafting the Municipal Act for local people to obtain self-government. The Hawai'i Territorial Legislature passed the act, but Gov. Sanford Dole vetoed it. The people were disturbed by the governor's action, and demands to control local government increased. Some 55 years later, the act led to Hawai'i statehood. Stewart was the first African American to practice before the Hawai'i Supreme Court. Between 1899 and 1904, he appeared before the court 16 times. (Courtesy *Hawaiian Journal of History*.)

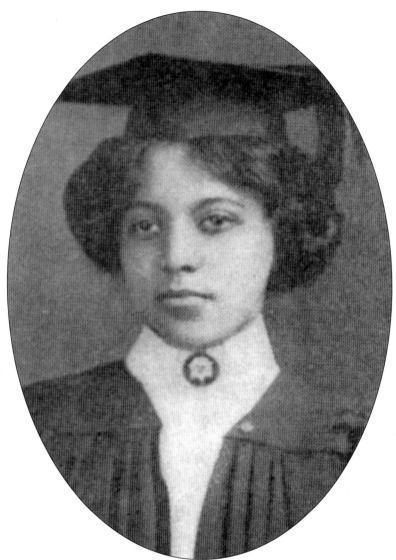

Alice Augusta Ball, scientist, was born in Seattle in 1892. She grew up in Washington State and Hawai'i. Her father, James P. Ball Jr., moved his family to Honolulu from Seattle in 1902 to improve the health of his father, James P. Ball Sr., who suffered from debilitating rheumatoid arthritis. The family lived in downtown Honolulu, and Alice attended Central Grammar School. James Sr. died in 1904 in Honolulu, and the family moved back to Seattle. Alice graduated from Seattle High School with excellent grades in science. She attended the University of Washington and graduated with two degrees, one in pharmaceutical chemistry and a bachelor of science in pharmacy. In 1914, Alice returned to Honolulu to study at the College of Hawai'i (later named the University of Hawai'i at Manoa), where she earned a master of science degree in chemistry in 1915. She was the first African American to graduate and also the first to teach at the University of Hawai'i. During her laboratory research, she discovered a breakthrough for Hansen's disease (leprosy) by extracting ethyl esters of the fatty acids from chaulmoogra oil. This chemical was injected into patients, and it reduced the symptoms caused by leprosy. The compound provided effective treatment for the disease. Alice suddenly became ill and died at the age of 24 in 1916. (Courtesy University of Hawai'i Archives.)

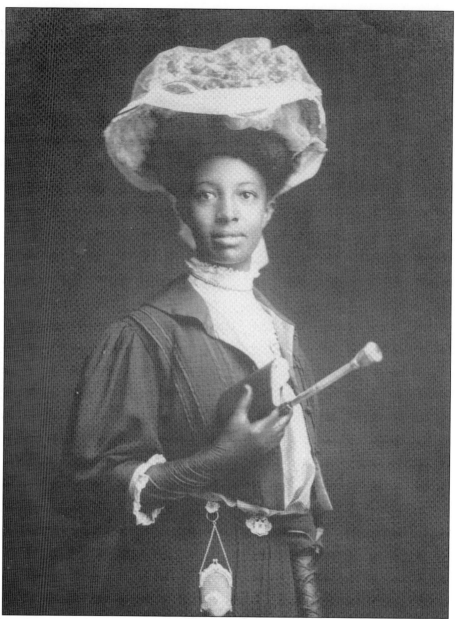

Carlotta Stewart Lai was 18 years old when she came to Hawai'i with her father, Thomas McCants Stewart, in 1898. She graduated from Punahou College in 1902 with a teaching degree. Carlotta was an elegant and distinguished African American woman. She was socially accepted, active in community activities, and enjoyed playing basketball, swimming, and dancing. Her first job was as principal of a common school on O'ahu. Later she was appointed to be principal of Anahola School on the island of Kaua'i, where she met her husband, Kun Tim Lai. They were married in 1916. The people of Kaua'i loved and respected her. She and Kun Tim did not have any children. Kun Tim Lai died in 1935 when he went to Hong Kong to visit his parents. The Lai family on Kaua'i was widely known and admired in the community. Carlotta and Kun Tim's sister, Ruth Ching, were very close friends. After her retirement as principal, Carlotta moved back to Honolulu, where she remained until her death in 1952. (Courtesy Moorland Spingarn Research Center.)

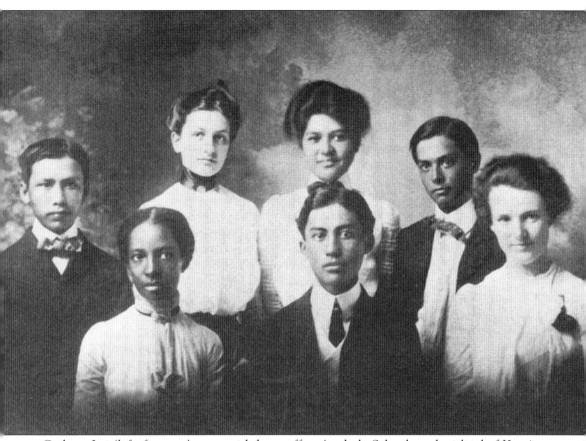

Carlotta Lai (left, first row) poses with her staff at Anahola School on the island of Kaua'i. (Courtesy Moorland Spingarn Research Center.)

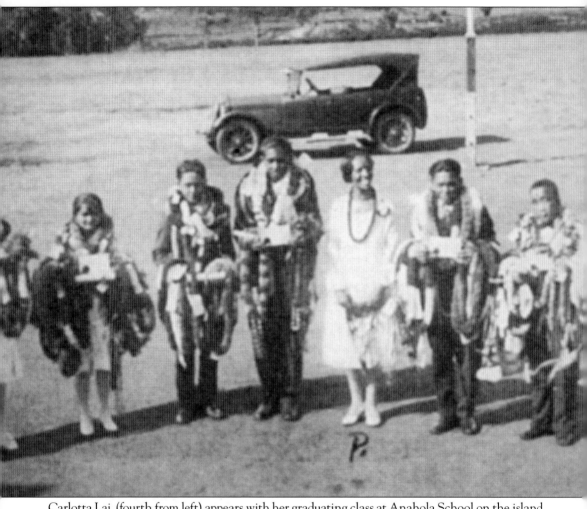

Carlotta Lai (fourth from left) appears with her graduating class at Anahola School on the island of Kaua'i in 1928. (Courtesy Moorland Spingarn Research Center.)

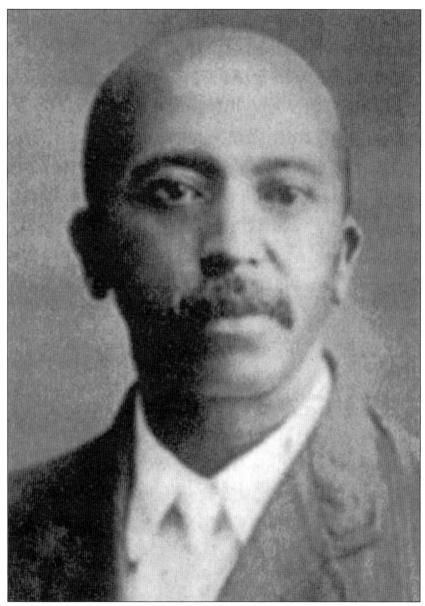

Dr. William Lineas Maples and his wife, Sadie, came to Hawai'i in 1901. Maples was hired by the Hawaiian Commercial Sugar Plantation in Pu'unene, Maui, to work in its hospital located on the northwestern side of the island. Dr. Maples's previous experiences and skills enhanced the services provided to plantation workers. He was instrumental in renovating the operating room and brought in the latest x-ray equipment and radium supplies that made the hospital one of the most modern medical facilities in the Hawaiian Islands. Sadie gave birth to two daughters, Elizabeth and Gladys, and her time was spent taking care of the girls. The people of Maui embraced the Maple family. In addition to utilizing his medical skills, Dr. Maples played musical instruments. He later founded the Navro Band that played in Wailuku Square on weekends and arranged the Pu'unene School song. Maples worked at the Hawaiian Commercial Sugar Plantation hospital for 30 years before his retirement. He died in Wailuku, Maui, on January 22, 1943. (Courtesy *Hawaiian Journal of History*.)

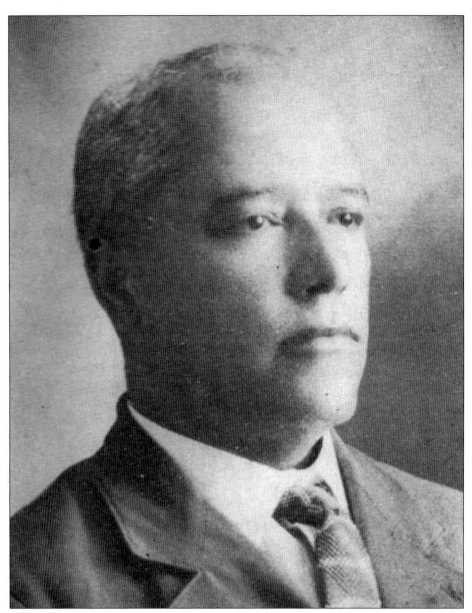

William F. Crockett, attorney, came to Hawai'i with a group of African American laborers recruited from Montgomery, Alabama. They arrived on the *City of Peking* ship on December 16, 1901. Crockett was hired by the Sprecklesville Sugar Plantation on Maui. He was responsible for supervising the black plantation workers and handling business matters for black recruits. When his contract was completed, Crockett established his law practice in Wailuku, Maui. He was appointed Maui district magistrate. Later he served in the territorial legislature for several terms. His wife, Annie, was an educator. She taught at the Wailuku Elementary School and was known as "Mother Crockett" to many local people. In her yard, she had a variety of plants and flowers. Because of her love of horticulture, she started to crossbreed the hibiscus with other flowers and was responsible for developing over 50 different varieties of the hibiscus flower that are seen throughout the islands today. The Crocketts had two children—Wendell Francis and Grace. (Courtesy Builders of Hawaii.)

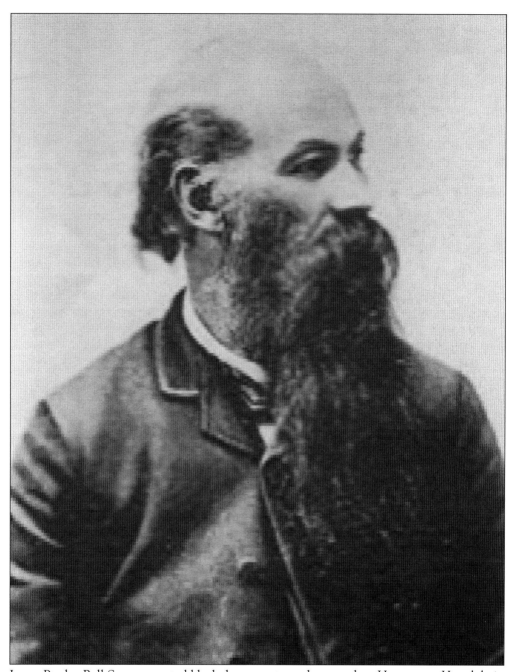

James Presley Ball Sr. was a noted black daguerreotype photographer. He came to Honolulu in 1902 to recuperate from rheumatoid arthritis. Ball was one of the first persons of African descent to learn the art of daguerreotyping. His son, James P. Ball Jr., was also a photographer and lawyer. The Ball family lived in Montana and Seattle before moving to Honolulu. James Sr. died in Honolulu in 1904. (Courtesy Montana Historical Society.)

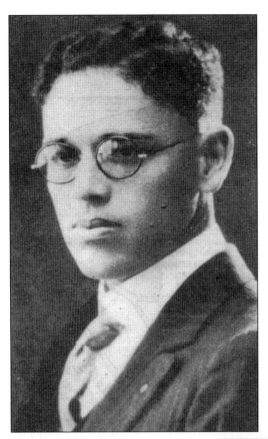

Wendell Francis Crockett followed in his father's footsteps. He graduated from the University of Michigan with a bachelor of arts degree in 1916 and a doctor of jurisprudence degree in 1917. Wendell was also one of the assistant editors of the Michigan Law Review. Three generations of Crocketts graduated from the University of Michigan Law School. Wendell returned to Maui to practice law with his dad. (Courtesy Builders of Hawaii.)

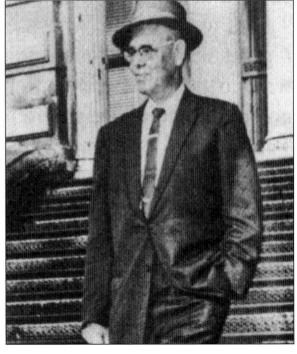

Wendell Crockett later served as a second lieutenant with the all-black 25th Infantry Regiment from 1918 to 1919 (*Honolulu Advertiser*). After his discharge, he returned to Maui and was appointed deputy county attorney on July 1, 1919. (Courtesy Builders of Hawaii.)

Two

Professional Blacks' Impact on the Island State

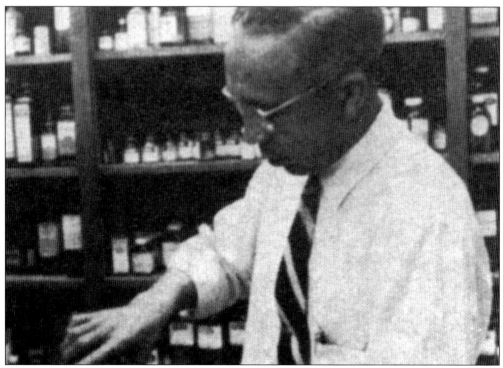

Dr. Wilber S. Wood was the first African American pharmacist in the territory of Hawai'i. While blacks in Hawai'i represent one of the smallest ethnic populations in the state, the vast majority reside near the two largest military installations—Pearl Harbor U.S. Naval Base and Schofield Barracks U.S. Army Base. Hawai'i is known for its culturally diverse people working and living harmoniously together. (Courtesy *Ebony* magazine.)

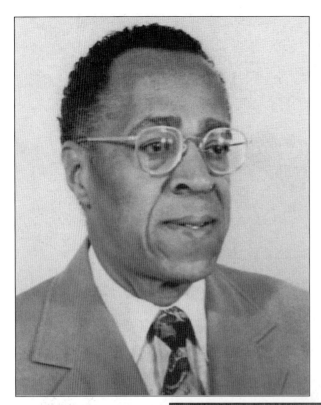

David H. Crowell was chairman of the Department of Psychology at the University of Hawai'i from 1958 to 1961. Crowell was instrumental in development of the Newborn Psychology Research Laboratory, a pioneering endeavor in conjunction with the Kapi'olani Children's Hospital in Honolulu in 1962. During that time, not much was known about the psychophysiology of infants. (Courtesy University of Hawai'i Department of Psychology.)

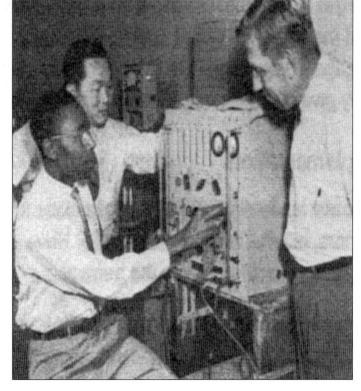

Engineer John H. Baker checks equipment at Pearl Harbor in the 1940s. Baker was one of hundreds of African Americans who came to Hawai'i as civilian workers in the 14th Naval District. World War II created a new labor market for African Americans across the nation as military service drained the supply of white male workers. (Courtesy *Ebony* magazine.)

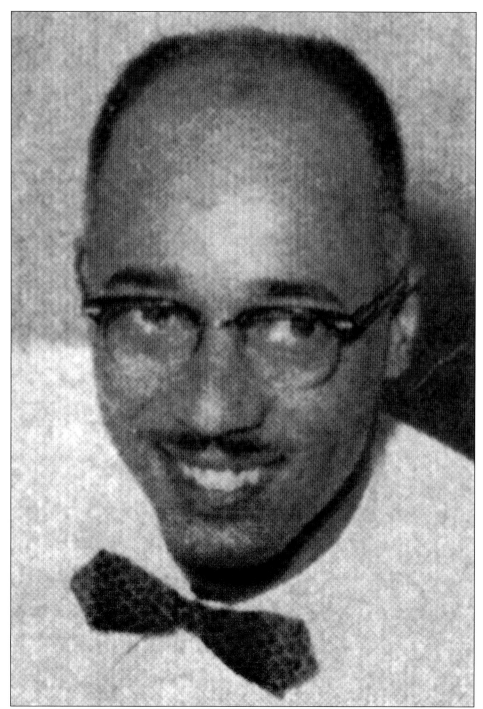

Ellis V. Ford was the training director at the Public Works Center at Pearl Harbor in the 1940s. He also taught a business course at the University of Hawai'i at Manoa. African Americans held supervisory positions in the 14th Naval District. President Roosevelt's Executive Order 8802 had created the Committee on Fair Employment Practice, which banned discrimination in hiring by defense contractors. (Courtesy *Ebony* magazine.)

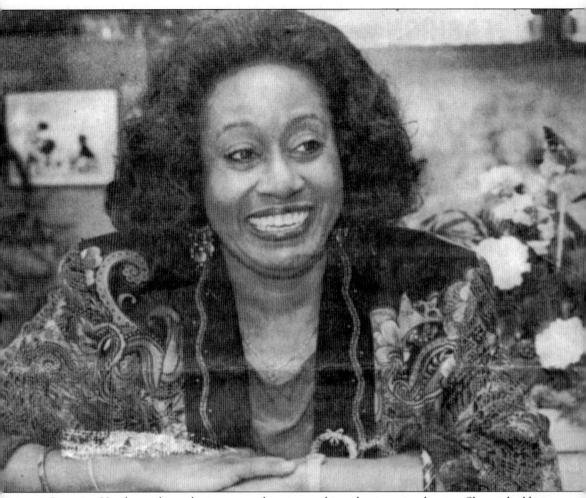

Lorraine Henderson has a doctorate in education and is a charismatic educator. She worked her way from being a classroom teacher to one of Hawai'i's outstanding principals. Henderson received numerous awards for her community service and is credited with turning a low-performing middle school in Kailua into a Blue Ribbon School. She retired after more than 20 years of service with the Hawai'i State Department of Education. (Courtesy L. Henderson.)

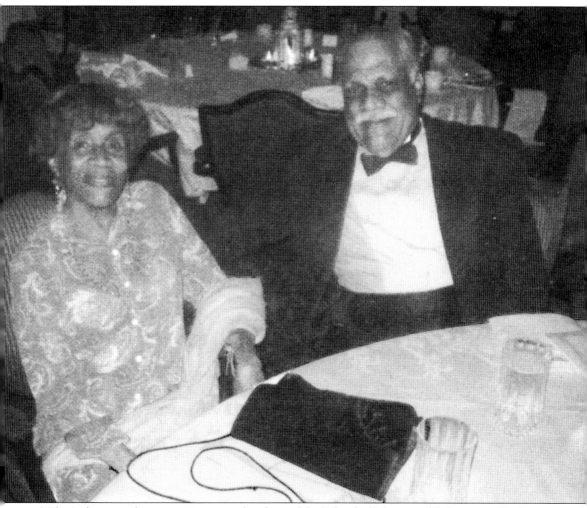

Miles Jackson, professor emeritus, served as dean of the School of Library and Information Studies at the University of Hawai'i. Jackson has authored two books and a documentary film about blacks in Hawai'i since his retirement (see acknowledgments). (Courtesy M. Jackson.)

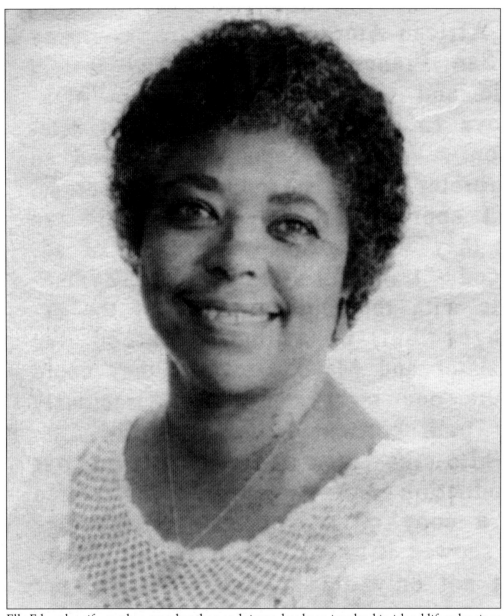

Ella Edwards, wife, mother, grandmother, and singer, has been involved in island lifestyles since her arrival in the 1960s. A professional singer, she has been actively involved with the Hawai'i Opera Theatre since its inception and has performed with the Honolulu Symphony Chorus as lead singer. Edwards has participated in many local organizations, including Alpha Kappa Alpha Sorority and The Links. (Courtesy E. Edwards.)

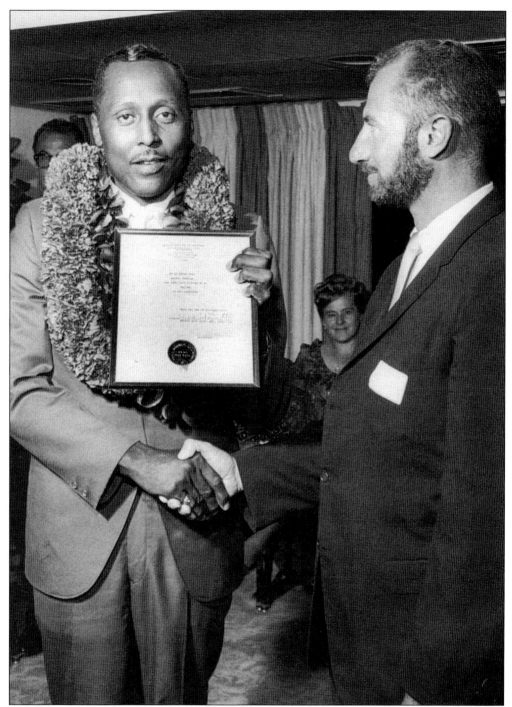

Alonzo DeMello came to Hawai'i in 1942 at age 18 from Chicago. He was hired as a civilian worker for the Department of the Navy at Pearl Harbor. He received a doctoral degree in psychology in 1970. The late mayor Frank Fasi appointed him to serve on the Commission of Children and Youth. DeMello developed a technique to improve study skills, enabling college students to master difficult assignments and improve their exam scores. (Courtesy A. DeMello.)

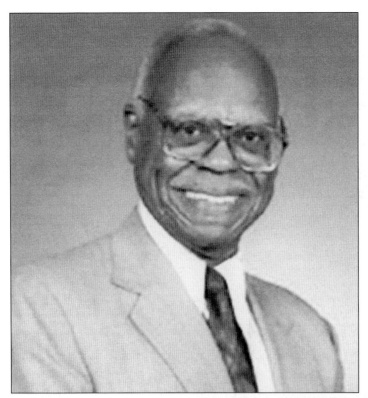

Entomologist Ernest Harris, Ph.D., is internationally renowned for his work on the fruit fly. He has worked at the U.S. Department of Agriculture for 40 years at the Biology and Ecology Research Unit, Tropical Fruit and Vegetable Research Laboratory in Honolulu. Harris has published over 100 articles in scientific journals and received numerous awards for his work. He resides with his wife, Bettye Jo Harris, on O'ahu. (Courtesy E. Harris.)

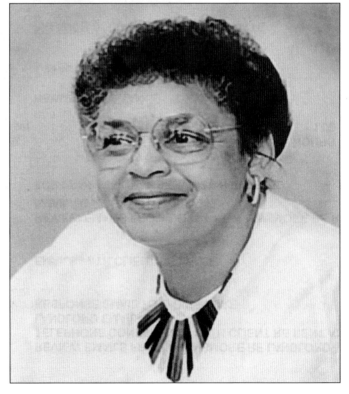

Donnis Thompson earned a doctorate and was the first women's track and field coach as well as the first female athletic director at the University of Hawai'i. She was also the first black superintendent of the State of Hawai'i Department of Education. Thompson was instrumental in obtaining and implementing women's rights in the historic 1972 Title IX federal education amendments legislation. (Courtesy D. Thompson.)

30

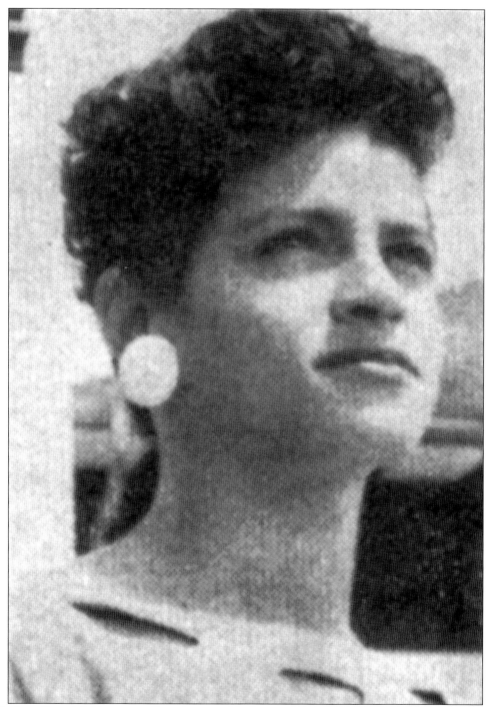

Barbara Crutchfield came to Hawai'i at age 23 after receiving a law degree from the University of Iowa. She taught economics and business classes at the University of Hawai'i. Crutchfield was one of the youngest attorneys living on O'ahu before statehood. In her classes, students felt comfortable participating in discussions, and the community welcomed Barbara into their homes and invited her to family celebrations. (Courtesy *Ebony* magazine.)

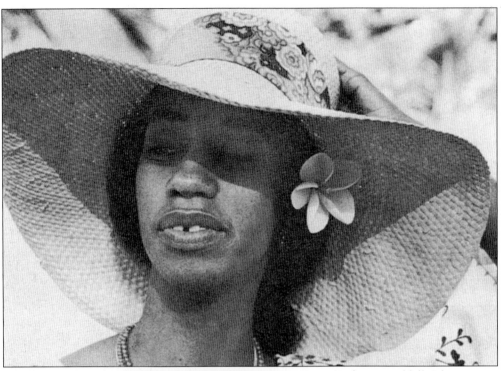

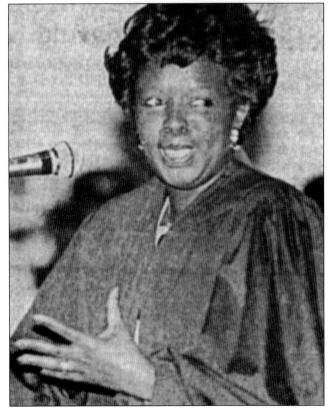

Kathryn Waddell Takara received her doctorate from the University of Hawai'i, where she was the first to teach African American courses. She is a poet and author of many books and other publications. Her father, Dr. William Waddell, was a veterinarian and a buffalo soldier who lived in Hawai'i until his death. (Courtesy K. Takara.)

Sandra Simms, an attorney, was the first female African American judge in the state of Hawai'i, where she served for 10 years. Simms worked for the Honolulu City and County Corporate Counsel before becoming a judge. She is a member of The Links and the Hawai'i African American Lawyers Association. (Courtesy *Honolulu Star-Bulletin*.)

Willie Bennermon, a dynamic businesswoman, has been contributing to civic life in Hawai'i and at Trinity Missionary Baptist Church for over 38 years. She is involved in community activities, including The Links and other sororities on the island. During the month of February, she volunteers at the Honolulu Academy of Arts with The Links to celebrate Black History Month. (Courtesy Trinity Baptist Church.)

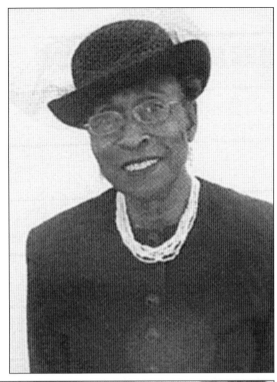

André and Daphne Wooten are attorneys who are involved in civil rights issues. Daphne served on the Hawai'i Civil Rights Commission and numerous committees in the legal community. Both are members of the Hawai'i African American Lawyers Association. (Courtesy A. Wooten.)

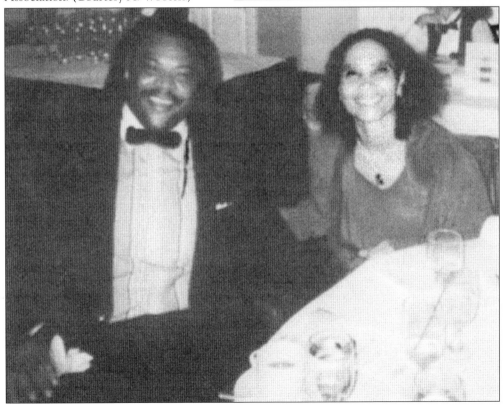

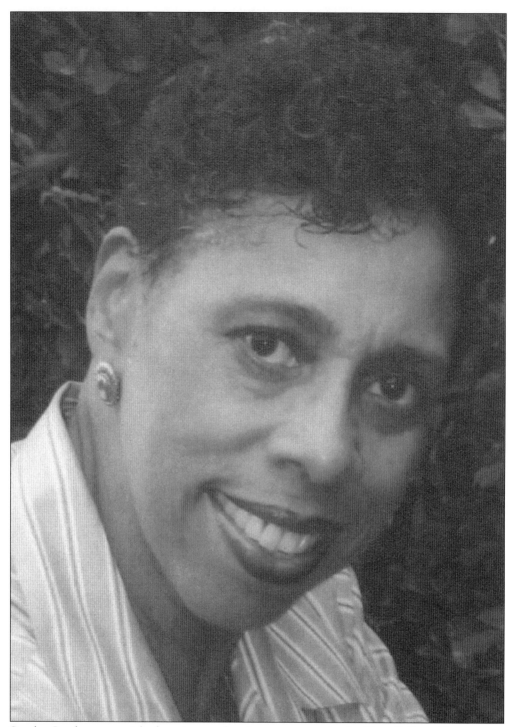

Sandra Sumbry, a special education teacher for many years in the Hawai'i State Department of Education, was one of the founding members of the Alpha Kappa Alpha sorority in Hawai'i. Sumbry has been involved with community organizations and assisting families of her special educational needs students for over two decades. (Courtesy S. Sumbry.)

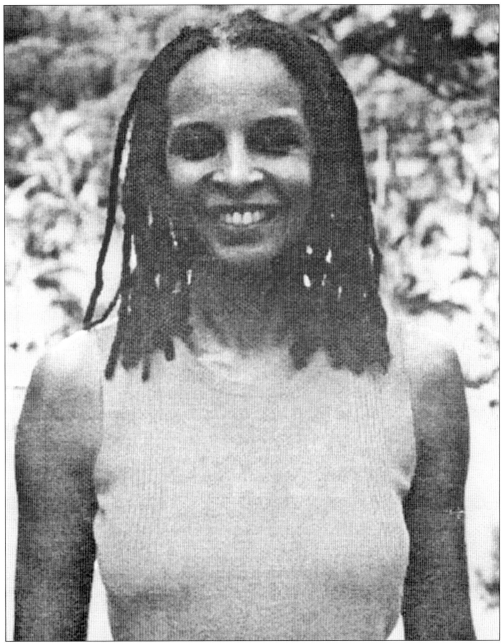

Jacqueline Langley, an assistant professor in communication at Hawai'i Pacific University, specialized in broadcast journalism and mass media. Langley developed the curriculum for visual communication at the university, and her students produced videos earning them awards that have been recognized by the Smithsonian Institution. (Courtesy Hawai'i Pacific University *Kalamalama*.)

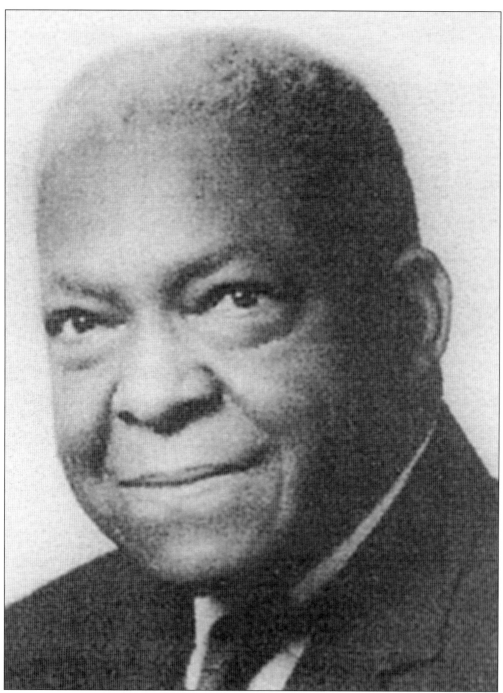

Dr. George M. Johnson, a renowned law professor, moved to Honolulu after retirement as dean of Howard University School of Law in Washington, D.C. He was immediately drafted to join with local attorneys and the late judge William Richardson in development of the University of Hawai'i School of Law that was named in Richardson's honor. After the law school opened, Johnson accepted a position as program director for preadmission and taught the first preadmission courses. (Courtesy *Hawaii Bar Journal*.)

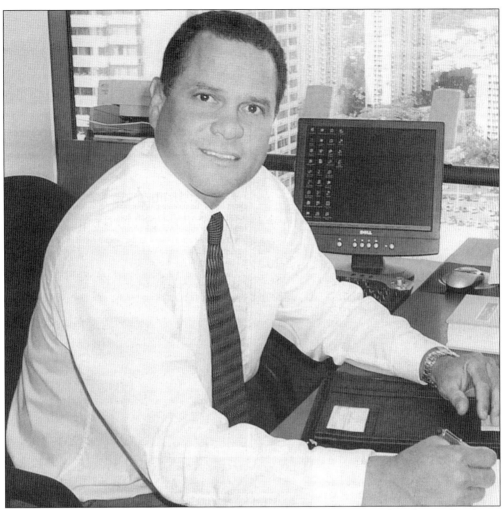

Attorney Rustam Barbee has been living on Oʻahu with his family for decades. Barbee has a reputation of being an effective attorney. He sits on the Supreme Court Lawyer's Discipline Board and participates in judicial retention committees. In addition, he teaches criminal law and is a member of the Hawaiʻi African American Lawyers Association as well as other local legal and community organizations. (Courtesy R. Barbee.)

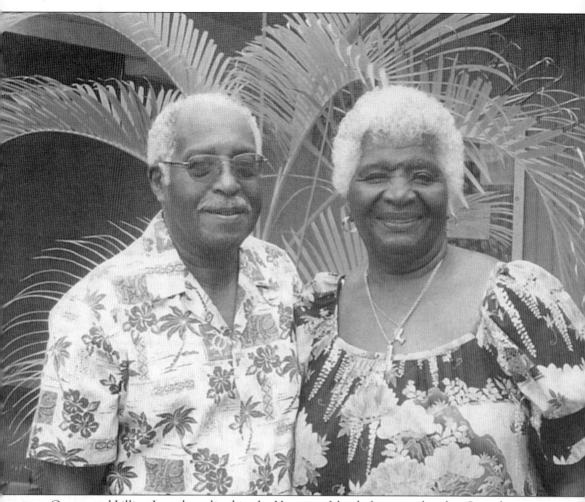

George and Lillian Long have lived in the Hawaiian Islands for many decades. Over the years, they have participated in numerous community organizations. The Longs are founding members of Trinity Missionary Baptist Church in Honolulu. Rev. Rubin Creel was the founder and pastor. The church began in Creel's home and was later relocated into a Quonset hut in Halawa. (Courtesy Trinity Baptist Church.)

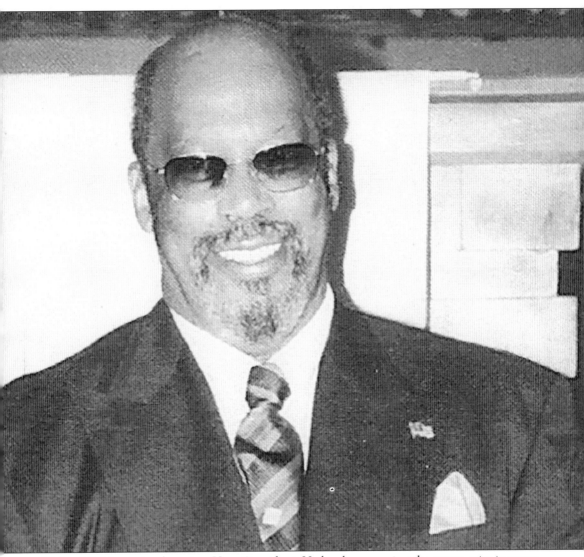

Richard Robinson is a longtime Hawai'i resident. He has been serving the community in many capacities, providing service to people in need. Robinson is a long-standing member of Trinity Missionary Baptist Church and participates in Masonic activities around O'ahu and in NAACP celebrations. (Courtesy Trinity Baptist Church.)

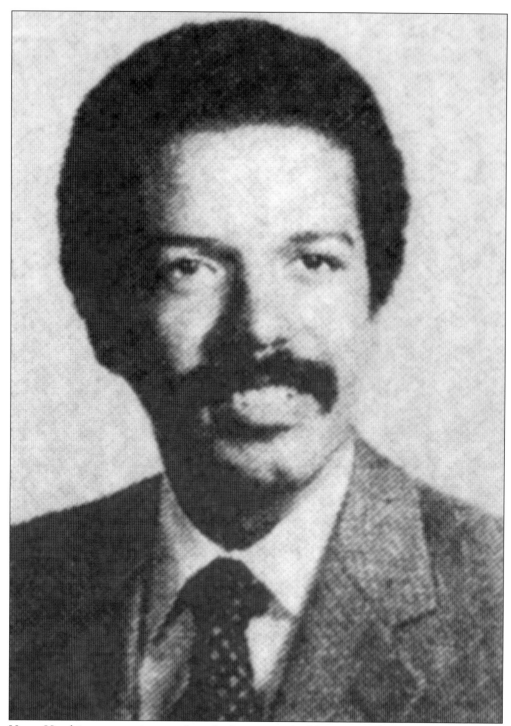

Harry Hutchinson was vice president for finance at the Hawaiian Telephone Company for a number of years. He served on community boards in the past and now plays golf for relaxation. Hutchinson encourages youth to go to college, take pride, and have confidence in what they choose to do in life. (Courtesy *Afro-Hawaii News*.)

Three

TERRITORY OF HAWAI'I POLITICAL AND MILITARY CONTRIBUTIONS

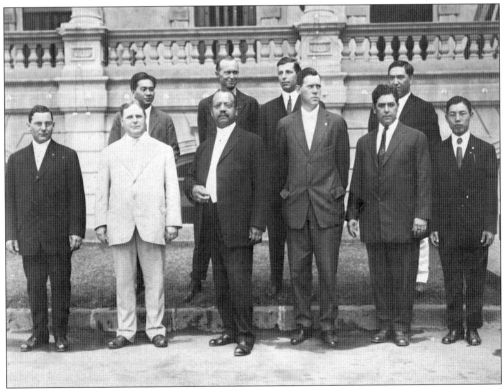

Charles A. Cottrill (first row, third from left), an attorney, arrived in Honolulu with his wife and son in 1911. He was appointed by President Taft and confirmed by Congress to be the tax collector (Internal Revenue Service) for the Territory of Hawaii. A distinguished, well-educated black man, Cottrill was interested in Republican politics and was welcomed by Hawai'i's Big Five corporations. They invited him to join several prestigious clubs and organizations. His son attended Punahou School, a private institution established by missionaries. (Courtesy Bishop Museum.)

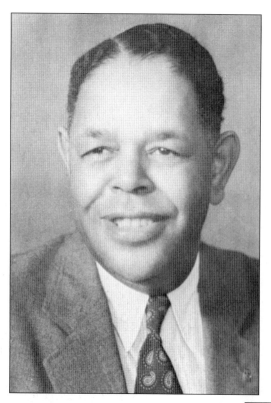

Nolle Smith, politician, statesman and businessman, moved his family to Hawai'i in 1915. He was the first African American to be superintendent for the Matson Navigation Company's docks, first assistant director of the Hawai'i Territorial Bureau of the Budget, and in 1920, the first African American governor of the Lions Clubs International, 50th District. Smith owned the first African American construction company in Honolulu, which was involved in building the Pali tunnels through the Ko'olau mountain range to the windward side of O'ahu. (Courtesy Bobette Gugliotta.)

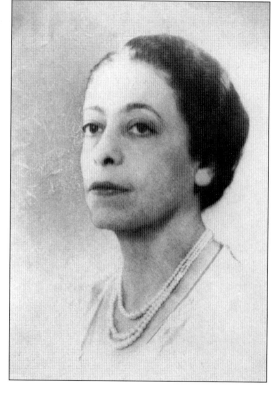

Eva Jones Smith, a classical pianist, met Nolle Smith in San Francisco before he came to Hawai'i. They were married in the Hawaiian Islands. Eva accepted the organist position at St. Peter's Church on Fort Street Mall. She also conducted an experimental kindergarten class at Kalihi Waena Elementary, the forerunner of kindergartens in the Hawai'i Public School System. (Courtesy Bobette Gugliotta.)

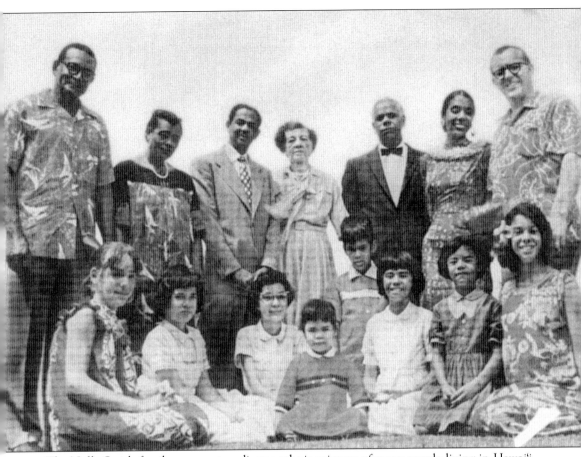

The Nolle Smith family represents a diverse ethnic mixture of many people living in Hawai'i. This family has embraced the host culture and its traditions and lifestyle. Today ethnic groups have added elements of their own cultures to local life. (Courtesy *Ebony* magazine.)

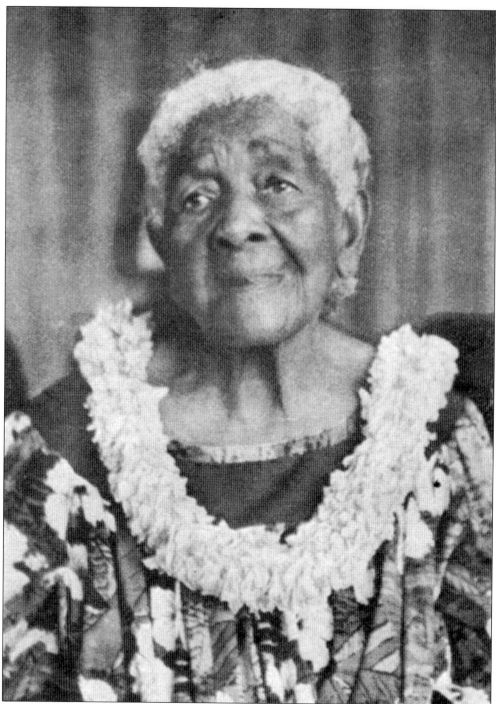

Melissa B. Smith was the mother of Nolle Smith. She found her new home an exciting place to live and immersed herself in the Hawaiian culture. Smith loved learning and cooking local foods for her family. Her culturally distinct neighbors were delighted to share their foods with the Smith family. Today there are four generations of Smith descendants living in the Hawaiian Islands. (Courtesy Bobette Gugliotta.)

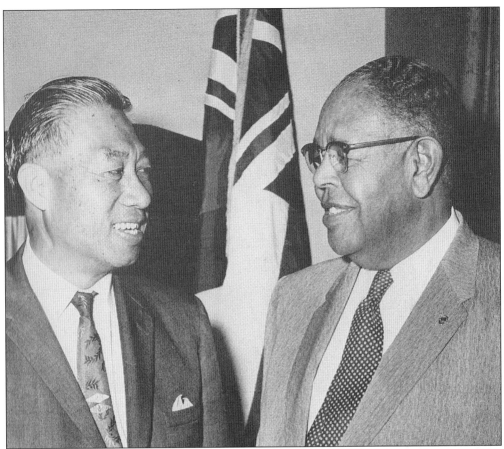

Hiram Fong (left) graduated in 1924 from McKinley High School in Honolulu with Nolle Smith's brother, Donald. Donald asked Nolle (right) to help his friend Hiram (later a U.S. senator from Hawai'i) find a job, as he needed money for college. Nolle found employment for Hiram and arranged with his business colleagues to give money to assist with his two years of college at the University of Hawai'i before he went to Harvard. (Courtesy Bobette Gugliotta.)

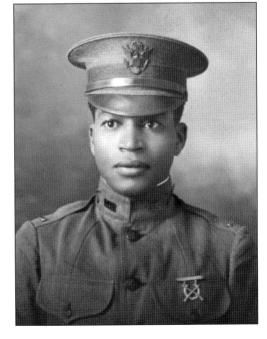

Lt. Clarence Ward found the people of Hawai'i very cordial and welcoming. In 1915, Company E of the 25th Infantry Regiment was sent to the Big Island (Hawai'i) to build a trail to the summit of Mauna Loa and cabins for researchers who were to study the volcano. Later the observatory was built. (Courtesy Char Collection, Bishop Museum.)

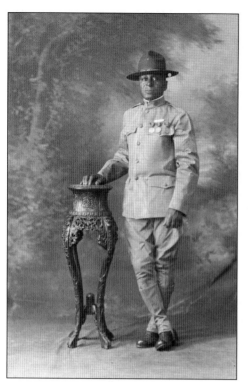

Sgt. E. P. Moss was assigned to the 25th Infantry Regiment and came to Hawai'i in 1913. The presence of thousands of black soldiers on O'ahu was impressive, and local people welcomed them into their community. The regiment was known in Honolulu for its outstanding baseball team and American-style boxing matches. (Courtesy Char Collection, Bishop Museum.)

Col. Chauncey M. Hooper was commanding officer of the 369th Coast Artillery, an African American regiment in 1943. His corps of New Yorkers called themselves "Hooper's Troopers" in Hawai'i. Undersecretary Robert A. Patterson (left) congratulated Colonel Hooper (second from right) for his unit's outstanding performance during his field visit to O'ahu in 1943. (Courtesy National Military Archives.)

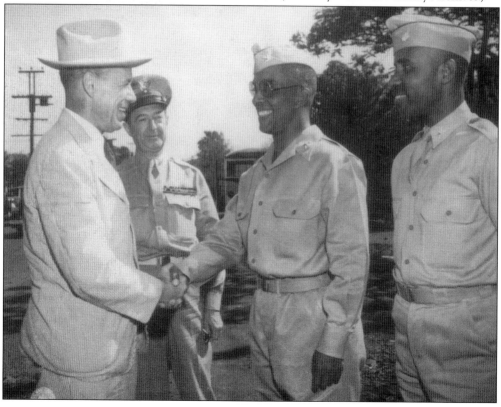

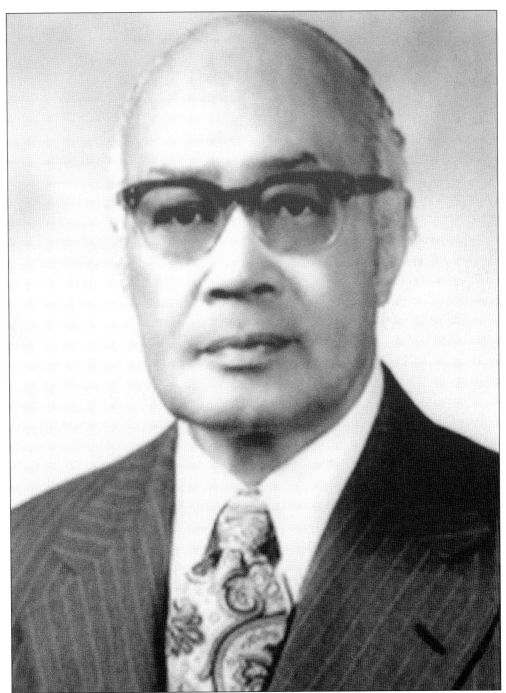

Thomas "Tom" Johnson served in the army USO in Hawai'i during World War II. He established and directed the USO Rainbow Club in Honolulu, which served African American service men. Tom was also overseer of all the USO clubs for African American servicemen. His staff consisted of local volunteer women from all ethnic groups. After the war, Johnson continued his education, earning a doctorate in 1967. (Courtesy Howard University Library.)

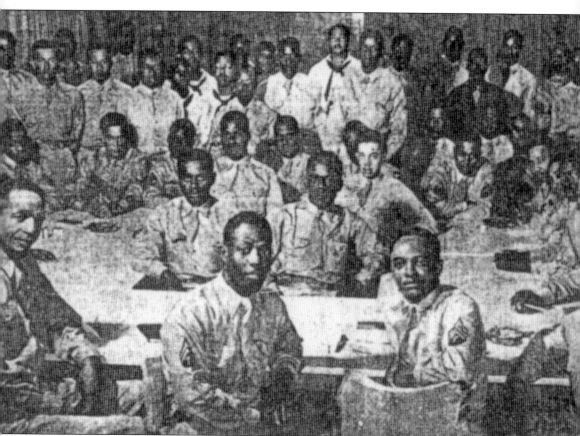

African Americans from various military units throughout the islands discuss the "Negro Problem" during a meeting at the USO War Workers Club in Honolulu in the 1940s. Tom Johnson, director of special services, is presiding. Thousands of black men were sent to Hawai'i during World War II. On military installations, black enlisted men were not allowed to socialize with white enlisted men in recreational facilities, thus Johnson established the USO Rainbow Club for black men. (Courtesy National Military Archives.)

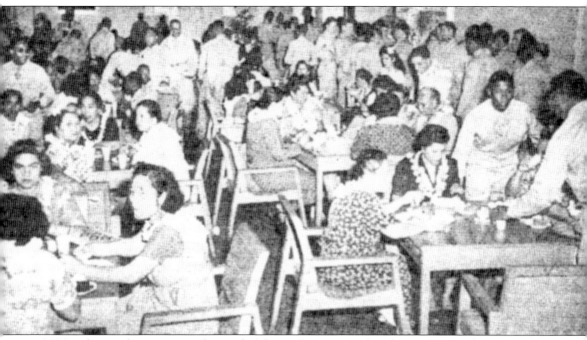

USO volunteer hostesses socialize with African American enlisted men. During the war years, the USO club's staff and volunteers were ethnically diverse local women. The atmosphere in these clubs was without strife and incidents. (Courtesy University of Hawai'i Archives.)

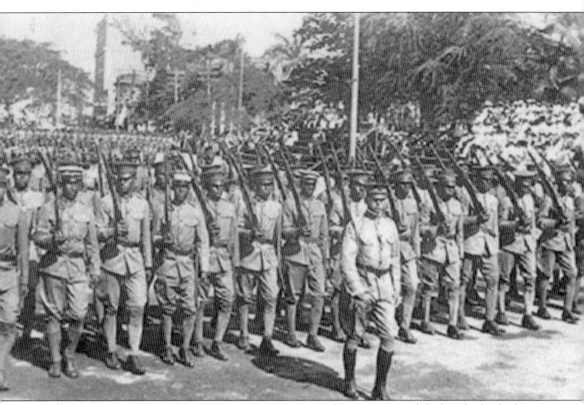

The 25th Infantry Regiment came to Hawai'i in 1913. In downtown Honolulu, hundreds of African American men are parading pass the 'Iolani Palace. Everywhere crowds of spectators cheered. People admired their musical band and precision marching in formation. The color guard was invited to serve at Lili'uokalani's funeral. Over 1.2 million African Americans served in World War II. (Courtesy Hawai'i Army Museum.)

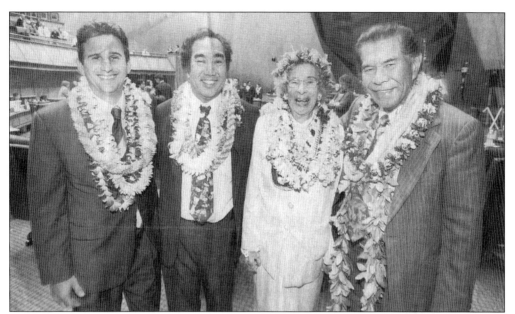

Helene Hale, a state representative from the Island of Hawai'i, is with her colleagues at the state capitol in Honolulu. A politician and teacher, Hale was the first African American to become mayor of Hilo in the 1960s. She was instrumental, along with the late George Na'Ope, in establishing the Merrie Monarch Festival, which brings tourists from all around the world to Hilo. (Courtesy *Honolulu Star-Bulletin*.)

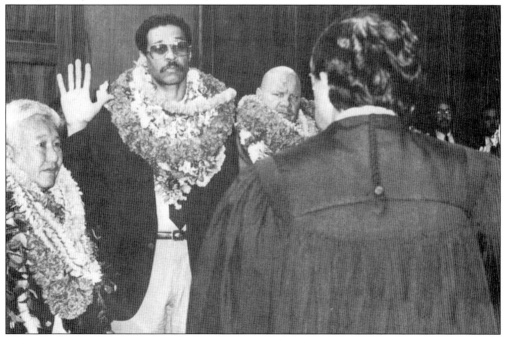

John Penebacker is sworn into office as a Hawai'i State School Board member. He is a graduate of the University of Hawai'i and a member of the university's Fabulous Five basketball team. Penebacker has been involved in political issues for many years. He lives on the windward side of O'ahu with his wife and children. (Courtesy *Honolulu Star-Bulletin*.)

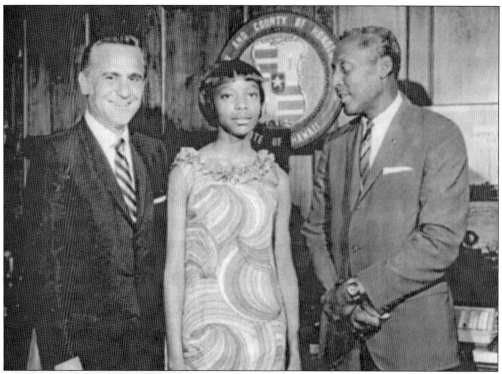

The late mayor Frank Fasi (left) is shown with Alonzo DeMello and his daughter, Lolita, in 1969. Fasi appointed DeMello to the Children and Youth Commission because of his work with adolescents in the Family Court and Koʻolau Correctional Center. DeMello has a soft spot in his heart for young people and always reaches out to them wherever he is in the world. (Courtesy A. DeMello.)

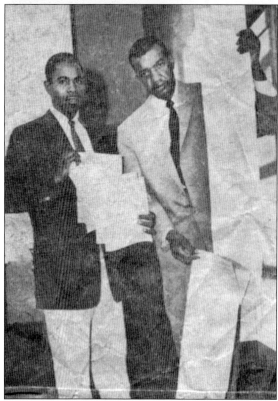

Clinton King (right), a minister, was the first African American to seek the U.S. presidency by filing papers in the lieutenant governor's office in the state capitol in Honolulu. Ernest Golden (left), the state chairman of the Afro-American Unity Party, is holding the petitions. It is interesting to note that, in the middle of the Pacific Ocean, blacks are active participants in the democratic process. (Courtesy EG.)

Dr. William Waddell was the first African American veterinarian to graduate and pass the Pennsylvania State Board of Veterinary Medicine exam in 1935. Dr. Waddell was a cofounder of the School of Veterinary Medicine at Tuskegee Institute (now Tuskegee University). He moved to Honolulu with his wife, Lottie Young Waddell, after his retirement. Waddell authored many books describing his profession and life experiences. Dr. Waddell was also a Buffalo Soldier and an active spokesman for the organization, addressing military audiences until his death. (Courtesy K. Takara.)

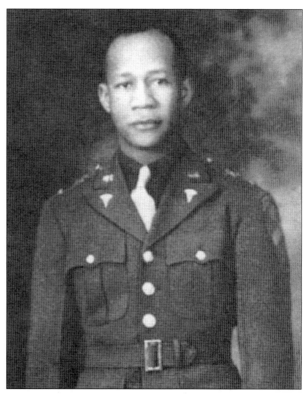

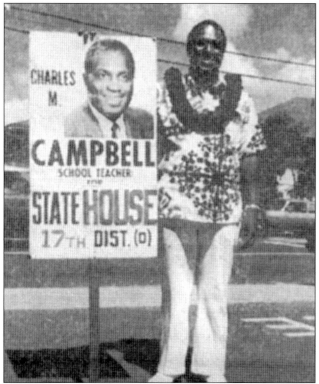

Educator and politician Charles Campbell was the first African American to serve on the Honolulu City Council. Campbell was the local inventor of sign waving, a tradition that has become a ubiquitous part of election season in Hawai'i. Campbell taught social studies at Farrington High School in Honolulu, where he encouraged his students to become involved in government. Campbell was also the first black to serve as a Hawai'i state senator. (Courtesy *Mahogany* magazine.)

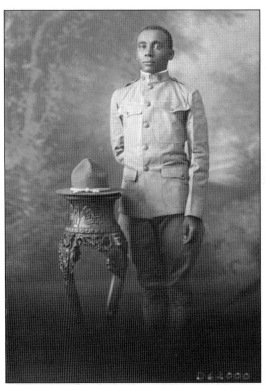

Leonard Lucas was assigned to the 25th Infantry Regiment and was sent to Hawai'i in 1913. Lucas was part of the E Company that was sent to build the Mauna Loa Trail and Red Cabin for scientists to study the volcano. The cabin remains today as a monument to those black soldiers who build the 18-mile trail up the rugged and hostile mountain in three months. (Courtesy Char Collection, Bishop Museum.)

During World War II, African American enlisted men often served as laborers. Their jobs were to load supplies on ships in preparation for the invasion against the Japanese in the Mariana Islands. Despite the hardships and second-class status of black soldiers, their role was important in every aspect of strategic planning to win the war. (Courtesy National Military Archives.)

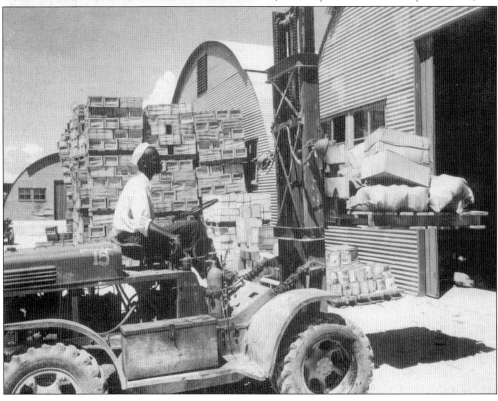

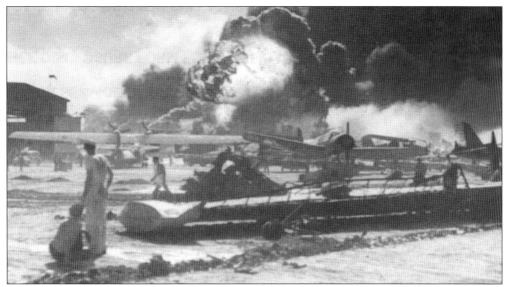

The West Loch disaster at Pearl Harbor on May 21, 1944, was a major maritime accident; hundreds of sailors, marines, and soldiers were killed. More than half who perished were young African American enlisted men. Those who survived were sent to the Mariana Islands, where they demonstrated their bravery, loyalty, and ability to support frontline troops. Oftentimes, they accomplished tasks without proper training. (Courtesy National Military Archives.)

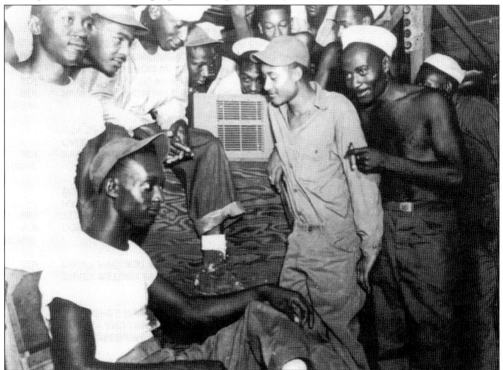

The West Loch explosion at Pearl Harbor was classified as top secret until 1960, and the men who died were nearly forgotten. After 66 years, the long-overdue recognition of these men was celebrated for the first time on May 21, 2010. (Courtesy National Military Archives.)

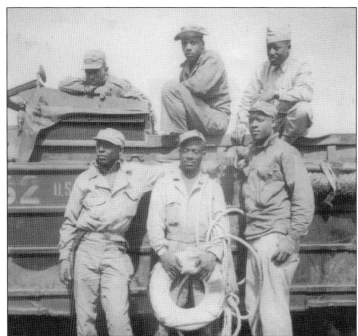

African American enlisted men's participation in World War II made significant contributions. Most black units in the Pacific were employed as service troops, but they also performed noncombat activities. Poor communication and lack of rapport with white officers often hampered their accomplishments and effectiveness. Nonetheless, their dedication and commitment to America's war efforts was unquestionable. (Courtesy National Military Archives.)

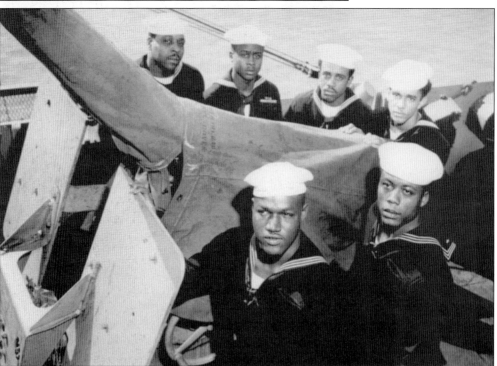

African American sailors' services in the war efforts proved to be an underrated asset in the Pacific. It was natural for commanders to want most of the limited passenger shipping capacity to be used to bring more combat troops into a theater, but service troops were vital for building the extensive facilities that were needed in combat. These men performed gallantly despite the indignities and prevalent Jim Crow attitudes of the time. (Courtesy National Military Archives)

Four

CIVIC AND SOCIETY LIFE OF BLACKS IN HAWAI'I

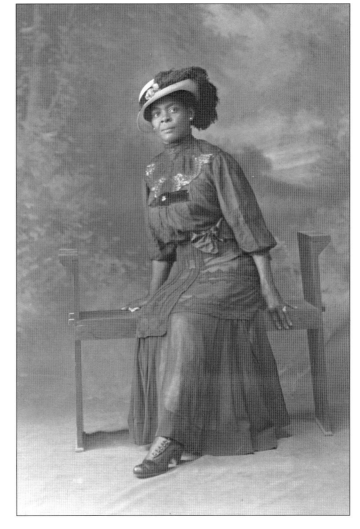

Elizabeth Brown was a community leader in Honolulu. This photograph was taken by On Char in his City Photo Studio in downtown Honolulu in 1915. African Americans participated in every aspect of the islands' ethnically diverse society. It was not uncommon to see black letter carriers, carpenters, and musicians around town. Also, on the island of O'ahu, the presence of black soldiers from the 25th Infantry Regiment was evident everywhere. (Courtesy Bishop Museum.)

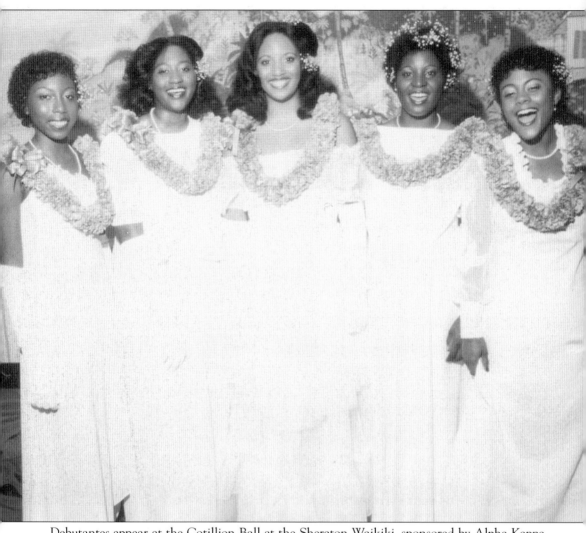

Debutantes appear at the Cotillion Ball at the Sheraton Waikiki, sponsored by Alpha Kappa Alpha Sorority Hawai'i. Cotillions in the African American community are a defining rite of passage into womanhood. (Courtesy DG.)

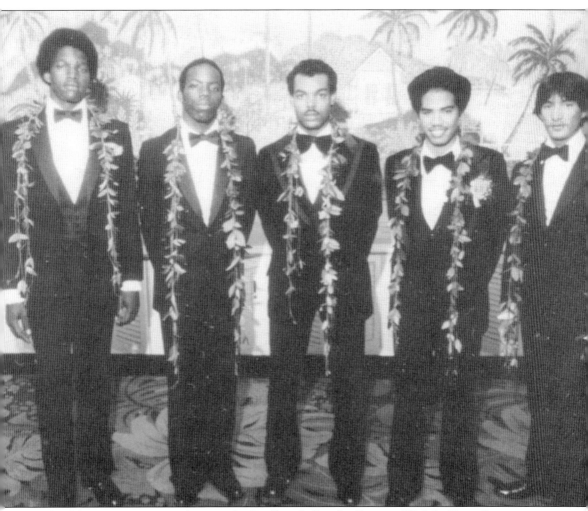

The debutantes' escorts are shown at the Cotillion Ball at the Sheraton Waikiki. Typically wearing tuxedos, younger male escorts accompany each debutante to the ball. (Courtesy DG.)

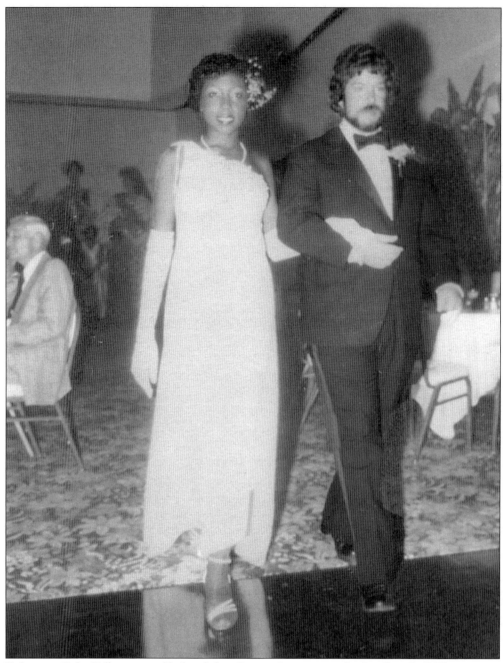

Debutante Delia Hill is escorted by her father, Steven Guttman, at the Cotillion Ball. The practice of presenting one's daughter to society is an ancient custom. It was essentially done to let all in the community know that a young woman had come of age. (Courtesy DG.)

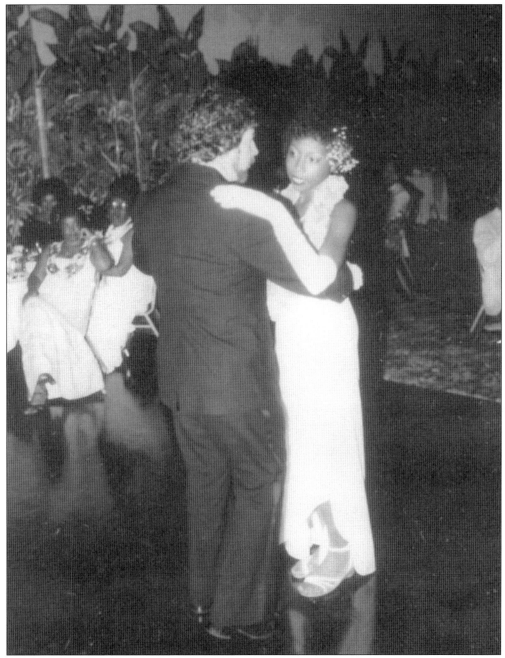

At the Cotillion Ball, Delia Hill enjoys the first dance with her father, Steven Guttman. A young woman participating in such an event represents chastity and grace in polite society. (Courtesy DG.)

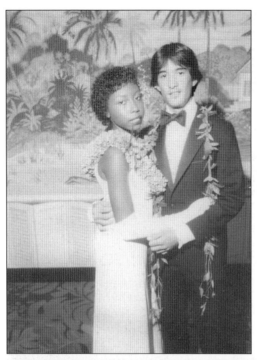

Debutante Delia Hill is shown with her escort, Ricky Aina. In today's cultural tradition, debutante balls in African American communities usually promote well-rounded young ladies with the focus on educational achievements rather than class status in society. (Courtesy DG.)

Delia Hill poses with her escort, Ricky Aina; an unidentified friend; and her sister, Gwen Hill (far right). The cotillion was a rite-of-passage ceremony celebrating the beginning of womanhood for young girls. Young ladies who participate represent different socioeconomic backgrounds. (Courtesy DG.)

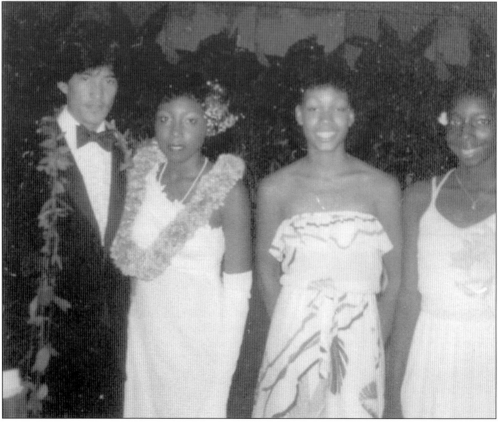

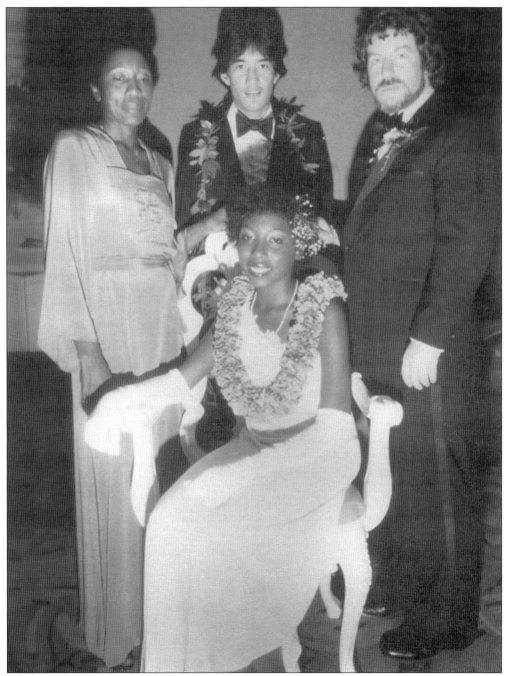

Debutante Delia Hill poses with her escort Ricky Aina and her parents, Deloris and Steven Guttman. In the African American tradition, celebrations are part of American history. (Courtesy DG.)

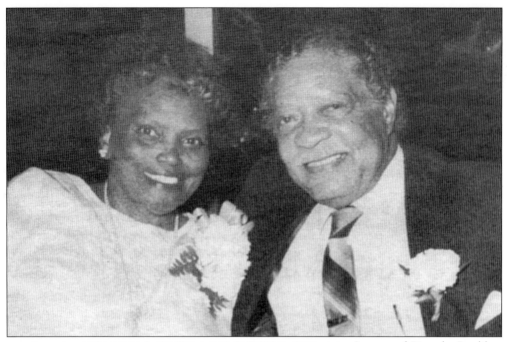

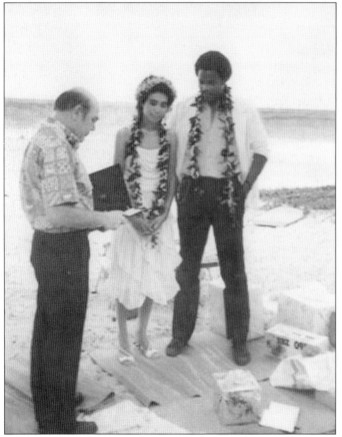

James and Dorothy Preddy arrived in the Hawaiian Islands decades before it attained statehood. They raised six children—Gail, Beverly, Pamela, James Jr., Gregory, and Michael. The Preddys were very involved in community activities. Dorothy was instrumental in starting the Wai Wai Nui Club and The Links. (Courtesy E. Jennings.)

André Wooten and Daphne Barbee are being married on the beach in Kaua'i. The Wootens are an integral part of the African American community in Hawai'i. As lawyers, they have made numerous contributions to the legal field. André is a competent surfer and videographer. (Courtesy A. Wooten.)

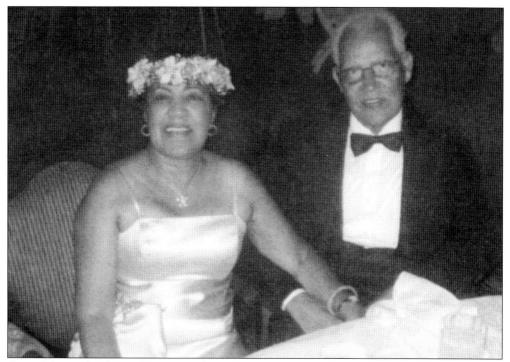

Gwendolyn and Albert Johnson are shown attending a formal community event. Gwendolyn is a public school teacher and classical soloist who sings at weddings, churches, NAACP dinners, fraternities, and sororities. She is also a founding member of the Alpha Kappa Alpha Sorority in Hawai'i. She and her husband are active in political events and community activities. (Courtesy *Mahogany* magazine.)

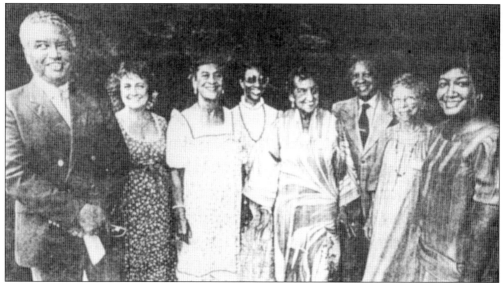

LeRoy King (far left), local NAACP president, poses with members of the executive board. King was also provost of Windward Community College. He and his wife, Arminta, were dedicated to resolving community problems and building a healthy relationship among local people. (Courtesy *Mahogany* magazine.)

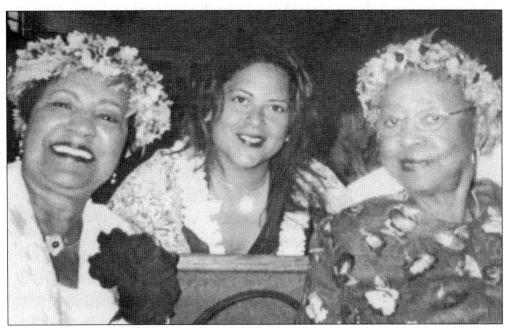

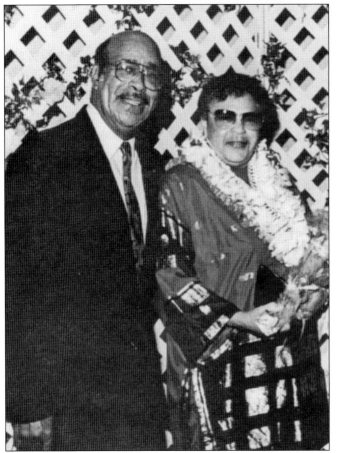

Gwendolyn Johnson (left) is with Maya Soetoro-Ng (center) and Bettye Jo Harris (right) at a celebration at the governor's mansion in Honolulu. Harris ran for political office and is one of Hawai'i's outstanding community leaders. (Courtesy *Mahogany* magazine.)

Artie McNair poses with his close friend Dr. Donnis Thompson. McNair is a classical pianist who has performed at many community events and senior citizens activities on O'ahu. McNair has been involved with the NAACP in Hawai'i for many years. He is known for his collaboration and communal aloha spirit in working with people. Everyone, particularly senior citizens, admires the work that he does. (Courtesy *Mahogany* magazine.)

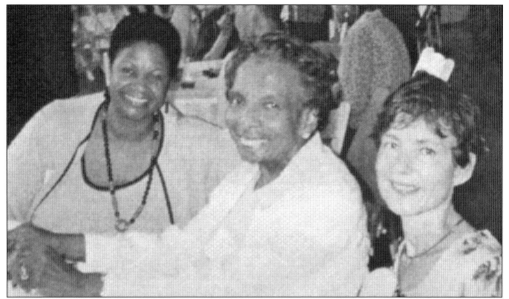

Sheila Callum (left) is pictured with Arminta James (center) and an unidentified friend (right) at the governor's mansion in Honolulu. They are attending a community event in Honolulu. Social events are occasions for the African American community to come together, since there are no black neighborhoods on the islands. There are several churches with large black congregations located close to military bases on Oʻahu. (Courtesy *Mahogany* magazine.)

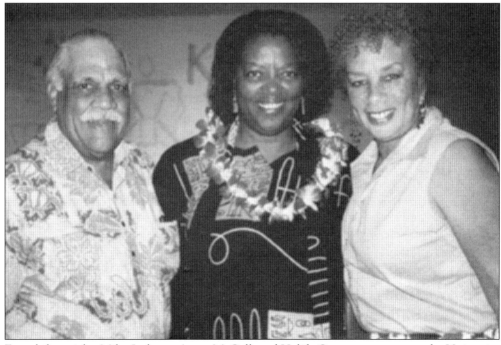

From left to right, Miles Jackson, Azure McCall, and Halifu Osumare are seen at the University of Hawaiʻi Black Institute celebration. Kathryn Takara was instrumental in getting the university to establish this event to recognize African American academic contributions to the islands. This event was in collaboration with the East-West Center. (Courtesy *Mahogany* magazine.)

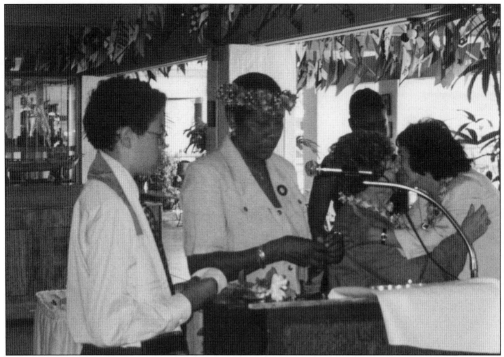

Seen at Alexander Guttman's bar mitzvah celebration with the Guttman family are, from left to right, Alexander; his mother, Deloris; his grandmother, Leah; and Auntie Rosalie. In Hawai'i, the Jewish community consists of many different ethnic groups due to intermarriages. It is not unusual to be invited to bar mitzvahs, one-year birthday parties, and Japanese-style 60th birthday celebrations, which are large family gathering in the Hawaiian Islands. (Courtesy DG.)

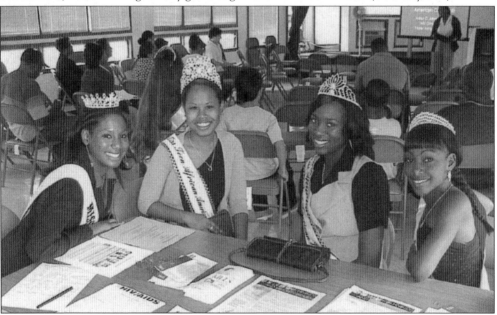

These Hawai'i Teen School Queens were honored at the Trinity Missionary Baptist Church. (Courtesy DG.)

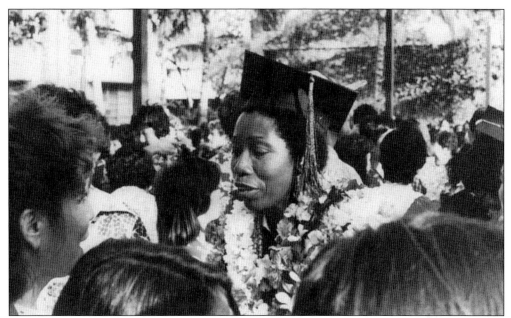

Deloris Guttman is shown at her graduation ceremony at the University of Hawai'i, where only about 1.4 percent of the over 20,000 students are African American. The majority of black students are athletes, participating in sports such as basketball and football. (Courtesy DG.)

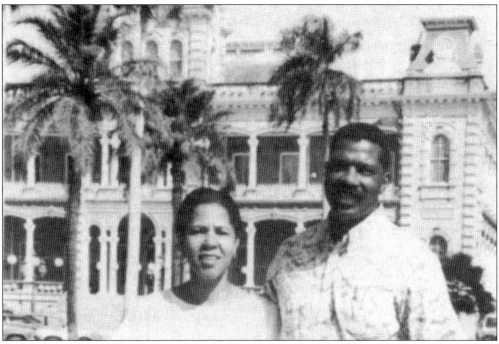

Paula Harris-White and husband, Ron Harris-White, are in front of the 'Iolani Palace. They produced the *African Hawaii News* and published *Black Pages*, a networking directory for African American businesses, professionals, and organizations in Hawai'i. These publications were used to communicate with Hawai'i's African American population throughout the islands. (Courtesy *Black Pages*.)

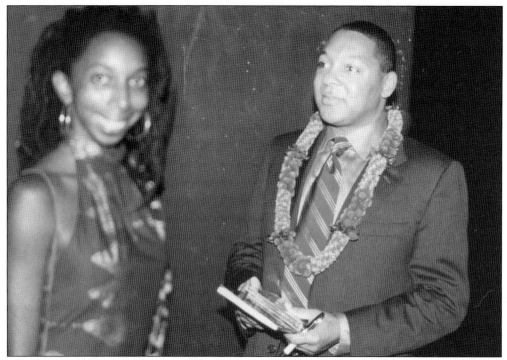

Gwendolyn Hill (left) greets Wynton Marsalis at the Blaisdell Concert Hall in Honolulu. The Honolulu Symphony brought in Marsalis for a special concert. While in the islands, Marsalis conducted workshops at several private schools. (Courtesy DG.)

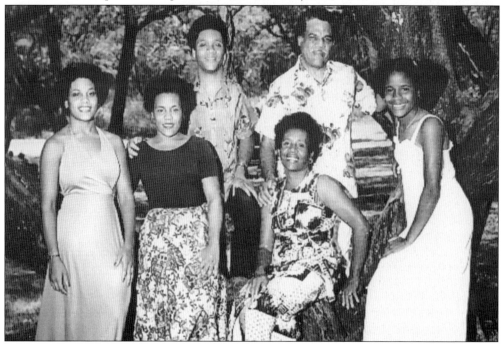

This photograph of the Jackson family includes, from left to right, (first row) Muriel, Marsha, Bernice, and Meila; (second row) Miles III and Miles Jr.

Pictured here is Elisa Joy White, who is an assistant professor of ethnic studies at University of Hawai'i. (Courtesy DG.)

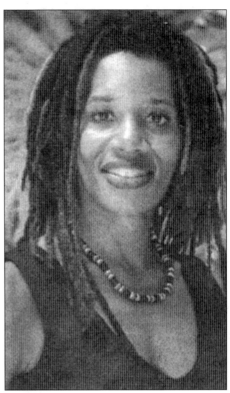

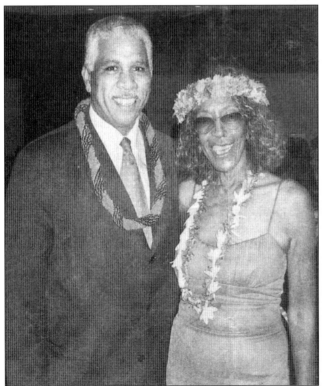

Faye Kennedy is at an NAACP dinner in Waikiki with Hilary Shelton, the guest speaker. Kennedy is an advocate and civil rights leader involved in politics and many local organizations. Her work with the American Civil Liberties Union is the platform that is used to confront issues in the community. (Courtesy *Mahogany* magazine.)

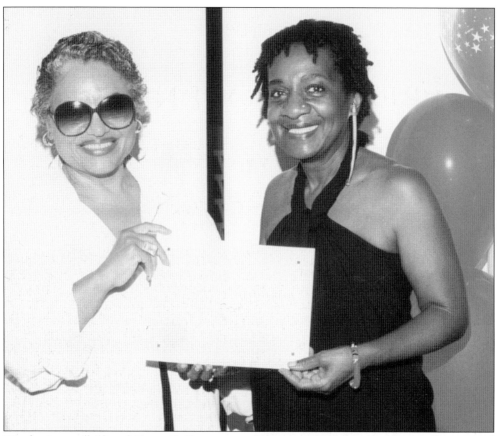

Marsha Joyner (left) and Durga Gaffney are at a Kwanzaa celebration. A political advocate and community organizer in the Hawaiian Islands, Joyner was one of hundreds promoting the Martin Luther King holiday. Gaffney was responsible for organizing Kwanzaa celebrations at the Hilton Hawaiian Village and Spa for several years. (Courtesy Durga Gaffney.)

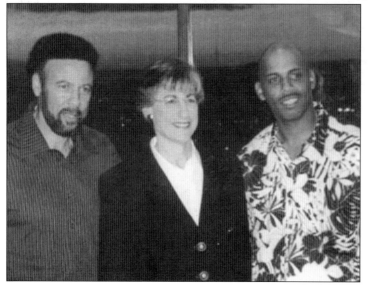

Governor Linda Lingle, shown here with Artie Wilson (left) and Darrick Branch, was a guest speaker at an event honoring our Kupuna Oka A'ina (elders) at the African American Diversity Cultural Center Hawai'i. (Courtesy DG.)

Five

FREEDOM JOURNEY TO HAWAI'I IN WORLD WAR II AND BEYOND

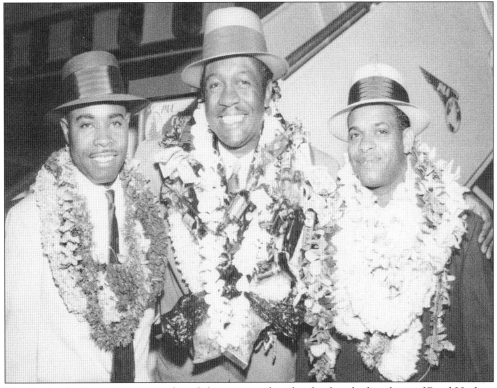

Hundreds of African Americans found their way to the islands after the bombing of Pearl Harbor. From left to right, Ernest Golden, Richard Harris, and Walter Mays arrived at age 19 from Athens, Georgia. Unlike their predecessors fleeing slavery, they were escaping Jim Crow laws. A need for civilian workers brought two young African American women, Lucille Mays and Clarissa Wildy, hired by the Department of Defense as clerical workers. Although the workforce and housing at Pearl Harbor were segregated, the Hawaiian Islands offered an opportunity to assimilate into Hawai'i's ethnically diverse communities. In downtown Honolulu, the most popular nightclubs were the Brown Derby Club, Two Jacks, and Swing Club. Mainland entertainers who performed in Honolulu included Dinah Washington, Billie Holiday, Erroll Garner, Paul Robeson, and Louis Armstrong, among others. (Courtesy EG.)

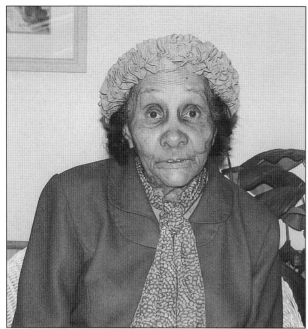

Lucille Mays was hired by the Department of the Navy to work at the Pearl Harbor U.S. Naval Base after December 7, 1941. She left her home in Virginia ready to explore the world. Mays met her husband in the islands, where she lived for many decades. After retirement from Pearl Harbor, the Mayses attended to the needs of people in the community through their church ministry. (Courtesy DG.)

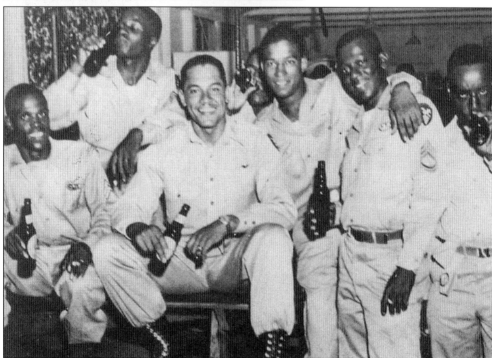

Unidentified enlisted men enjoy a beer after work at the USO. The USO clubs established for black military personnel provided a noncombative environment for these young men to socialize. Military commanders often had a difficult time preventing fights between black and white personnel. Thousands of military men on the island of Oʻahu brought their prejudices and biases with them. It was difficult for them to live harmoniously in such close proximity to each other. (Courtesy the National Military Archives.)

Ernest Golden (left) and Milton Jordan are walking in downtown Honolulu. Golden said anything one wanted could be found in the area—dance halls, nightclubs, pool halls, booze, and women. When the weekend came, civilian and military personnel headed for downtown Honolulu. Everything they needed for entertainment, they found in town. During the war years, downtown was where the action took place. (Courtesy EG.)

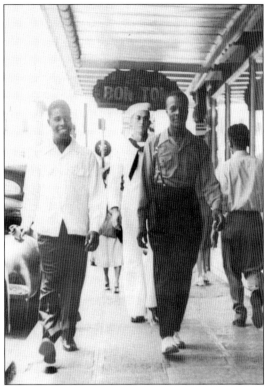

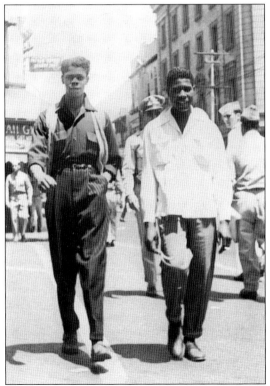

Johnny Cunningham (left) and Ernest Golden are enjoying a Saturday afternoon on Fort Street in downtown Honolulu. From Chinatown to Nuuanu Avenue, businesses were packed with sailors and soldiers of all ethnic groups. Some venues were even segregated because white men did not want to socialize in the same venue as the blacks. Nevertheless, Honolulu, like other places around the world, had every vice possible available. (Courtesy EG.)

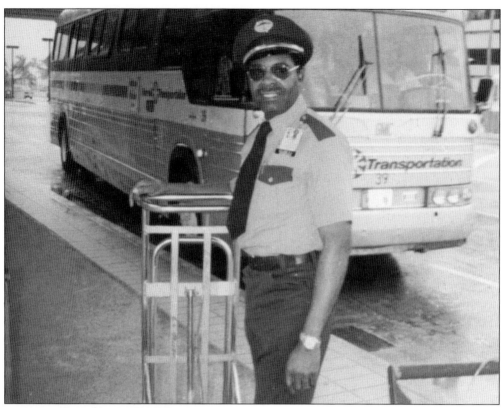

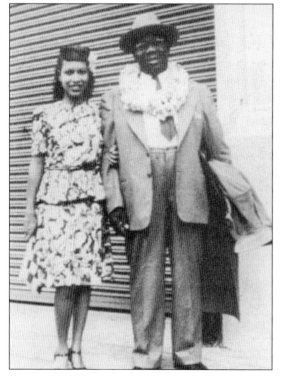

Ernest Golden was a man of many talents. He was a bus driver for the Honolulu Rapid Transit, a skycap, bellhop, and an airport concessionaire. When his civil service worker's contract expired, Golden became a Hawai'i resident. A person had to be innovative to create work, since most jobs available were at Pearl Harbor. There were limited job possibilities in the community during those years. (Courtesy EG.)

Clarissa Wildy welcomes her dad at the Honolulu airport with a lei. During the 1940s, the flight across the Pacific Ocean took many more hours than today. Pan Am Clipper Service was the only air route to the islands. In those days, it was a luxury to be able to visit the Hawaiian Islands. (Courtesy DG.)

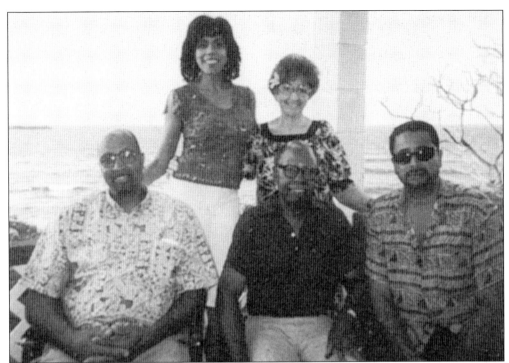

The Golden family, shown here from left to right, includes (first row) Carl, Ernest, and Kevin; (second row) Karen and Evangeline. Their eldest son, Keith, lives in Utah. Ernest purchased a home on the windward side of Oʻahu on Laʻie Point, which juts out into the Pacific. The view from his home was unobstructed in the 1950s, when he raised his children. The luscious, green, Hawaiian setting surrounding his home was picturesque. (Courtesy EG.)

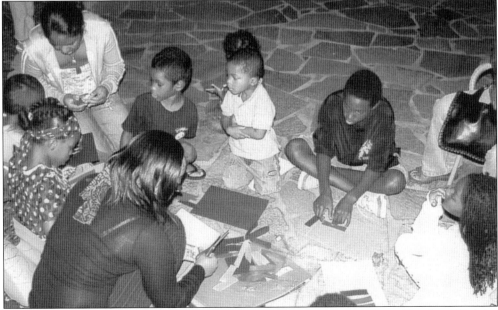

These children are celebrating Kwanzaa at the Hilton Hawaiian Village Hotel in Waikiki. (Courtesy DG.)

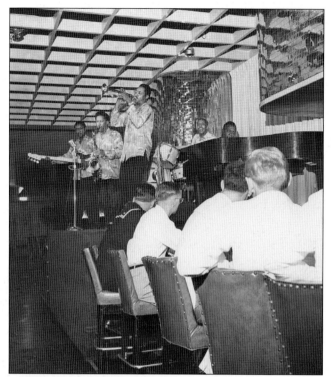

This African American band was playing music at an officers' military club in Honolulu. In military clubs, black bands provided most of the entertainment. In that era, similar to the Cotton Club in Harlem, most work black entertainers found was in white establishments. (Courtesy *New Pacific* magazine.)

The Nat King Cole Trio performed at Lau Yee Chai's Restaurant in Waikiki in the 1940s. The war years were very lucrative for black entertainers in Hawai'i. There were several outstanding clubs that brought the likes of Billie Holiday, Dinah Washington, and other well-known performers to the islands. (Courtesy EG.)

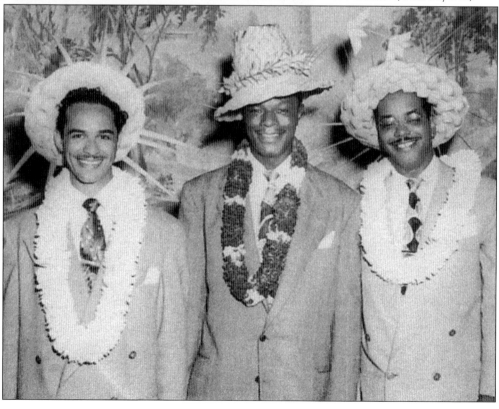

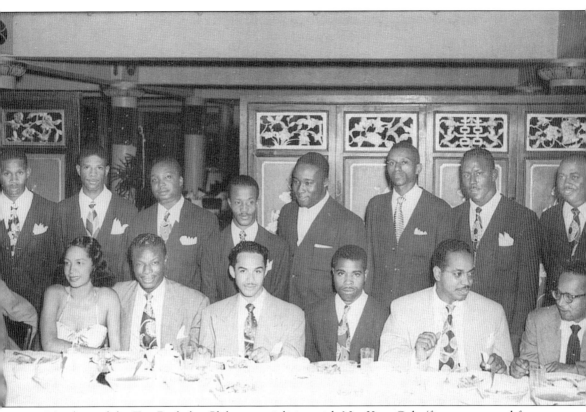

Members of the Ten Bachelor Club are socializing with Nat King Cole (first row, second from left) at Lau Yee Chai's Restaurant. Ernest Golden (first row, third form right) and ten of his single friends formed this private social club to entertain female guests and give the men an opportunity to meet and date local girls. The club became known for its great parties. Hosting the Nat King Cole Trio in a concert in Honolulu was the highlight of the club's social life. Gradually the guys got married and the group dwindled and then dissolved. (Courtesy EG.)

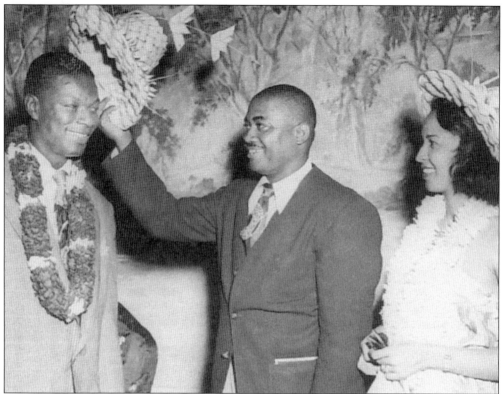

Nat King Cole (left) is given a lauhala hat by John Howell, a member of the Ten Bachelor Club. Howell's wife presented Cole with a lei. Upon arrival at the Honolulu airport, the custom was to greet everyone with a lei. At formal events, leis presented to guests are a way to say welcome and aloha. (Courtesy EG.)

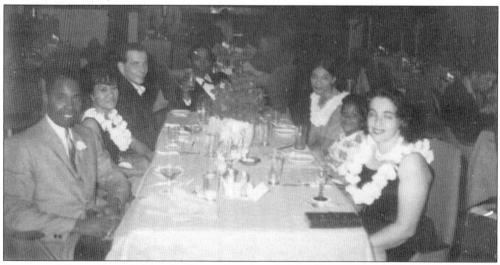

Ernest and Evangeline Golden (left) are shown with friends at a Honolulu club. Nightlife in Hawai'i was not any different than back home, and friends always congregated at their favorite nightspots. Black people, during the war years, were relegated to live in one area whether they were civilians or military personnel. (Courtesy EG.)

A group of skycaps enjoy an evening after work at a nightclub in downtown Honolulu. Thousands of military and civilian men found entertainment in the bars and dance halls during World War II. (Courtesy EG.)

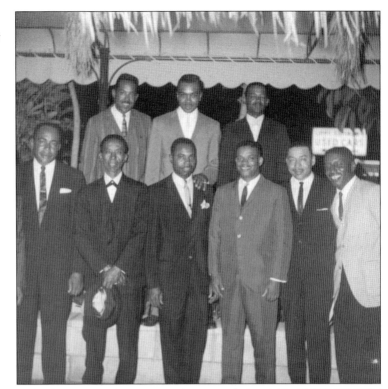

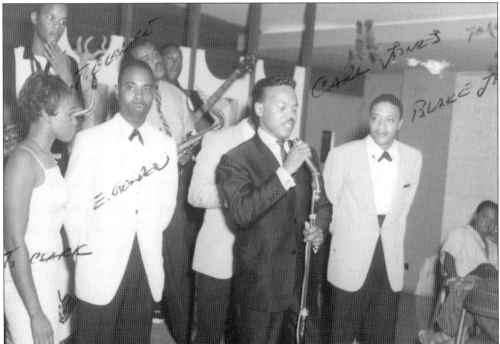

The Gold Tones Singers are seen performing at the Hawaiian Lanes Club in Honolulu. When there is limited entertainment in a neighborhood, people create it. Thus these singers became part of the cabaret scene in Honolulu for black people. (Courtesy EG.)

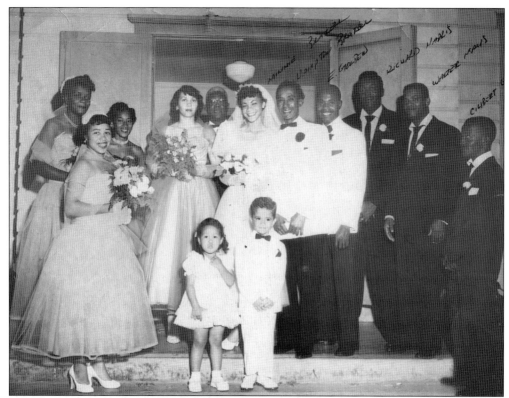

Hampton and Minnie Brazell's wedding party poses for this photograph in Honolulu. The Brazell wedding was a most spectacular occasion in Honolulu during the 1950s. Minnie worked at Hickam Air Force Base. Hampton was from San Francisco. The Honolulu Airport Skycap service was his business venture. They met in Honolulu. (Courtesy EG.)

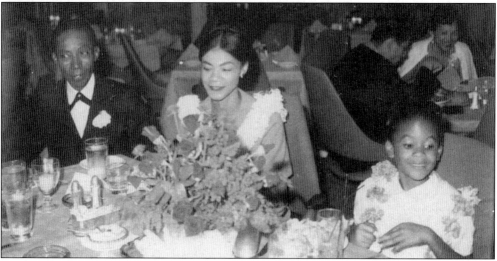

Newlyweds Hampton and Minnie Brazell and their unidentified flower girl are shown at their wedding dinner. This extravaganza was attended by most black people on the island of O'ahu. The Brazells purchased a home not far from Pearl Harbor in the Aiea community, where they raised their children. (Courtesy EG.)

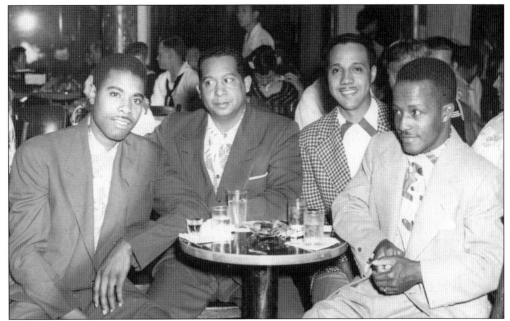

Ernest Golden (far left) was with unidentified friends at a nightclub. Ernest was a debonair young man who always brought people together. He even opened his own club in the McCully neighborhood, not far from Waikiki. Everyone knew this young man. (Courtesy EG.)

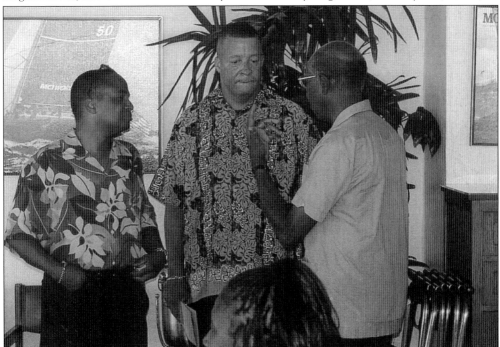

From left to right, Seibert Murphy, Bishop Michael Henderson, and Ernest Golden met at the Waikiki Yacht Club in Honolulu for a combined chamber of commerce and African American Diversity Cultural Center Hawai'i meeting. These meetings brought black people together to discuss community events and planning. (Courtesy DG.)

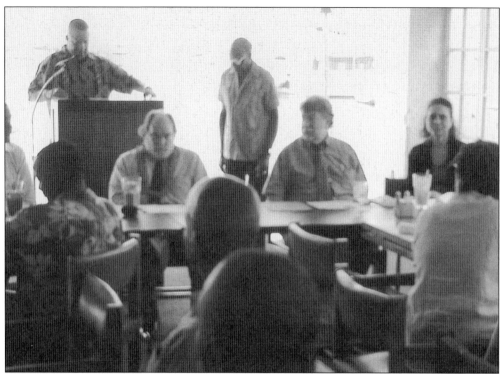

Bishop Michael Henderson is blessing the meeting of the Waikiki Yacht Club with former congressman Neil Abercrombie, who was the keynote speaker. Abercrombie has always encouraged people of African descent to become involved in political issues. Although many blacks are associated with the military, few are interested in political office. The fact that there is no predominantly black neighborhood could be a reason for lack of involvement. (Courtesy DG.)

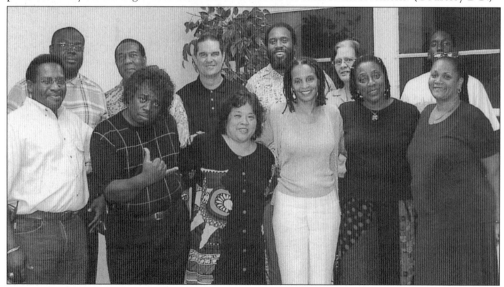

This is an African American Chamber Commercial Council Hawai'i holiday party. The black chamber represents small businesses of ethnic diversity and offers them networking and social opportunities. (Courtesy DG.)

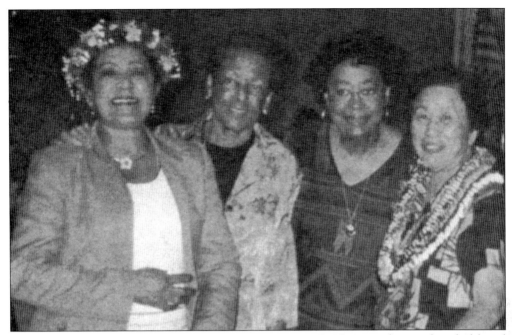

From left to right, Gwen Johnson, Winnie Simmons, Bettye Jo Harris, and an unidentified friend attend a community event. These occasions afford black people an opportunity to socialize and get to know each other. In some neighborhoods it was rare to find two or three black families living in the area. (Courtesy *Mahogany* magazine.)

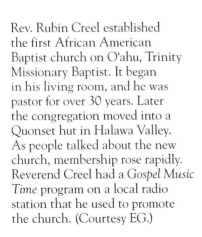

Rev. Rubin Creel established the first African American Baptist church on Oʻahu, Trinity Missionary Baptist. It began in his living room, and he was pastor for over 30 years. Later the congregation moved into a Quonset hut in Halawa Valley. As people talked about the new church, membership rose rapidly. Reverend Creel had a *Gospel Music Time* program on a local radio station that he used to promote the church. (Courtesy EG.)

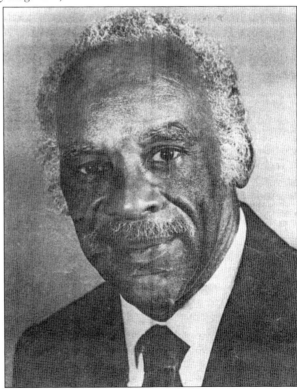

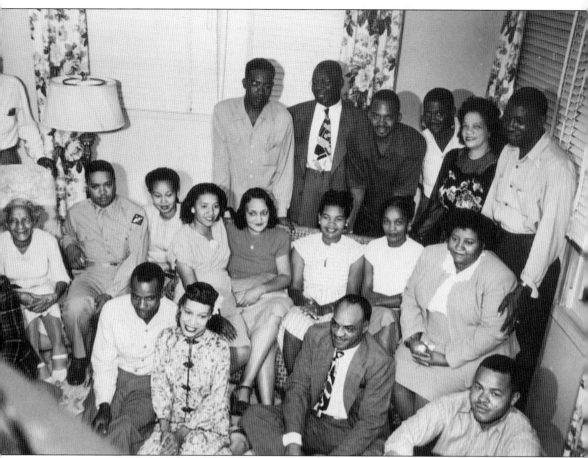

Clarissa and Marion Wildy (both sitting at far left on the floor in the first row) socialize with friends in their home in the Civilian Housing Area III at Pearl Harbor. Both Clarissa and Marion were civilian workers at the Navy 14th District. Since socializing was limited in the community for African Americans, particularly women, it was natural for friends to meet in homes. Marion was an avid golfer, winning numerous awards over the years. In addition, he taught bridge classes to tourists at Waikiki hotels in the evening. The Wildys were seen in an *Ebony* article about blacks in the territory of Hawai'i. (Courtesy *Ebony* magazine.)

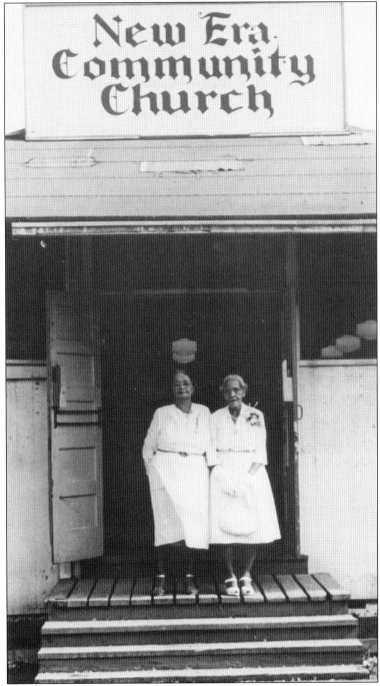

The New Era Community Church was located in the Pearl Harbor Civilian Housing Area III. Evangeline and Ernest Golden were married there on November 23, 1950. During that time, most African Americans attended the New Era Community Church because many churches were segregated and operated by white ministers. Today the original building has been renovated and has become part of the existing facilities at Trinity Missionary Baptist Church. (Courtesy University of Hawai'i Archives.)

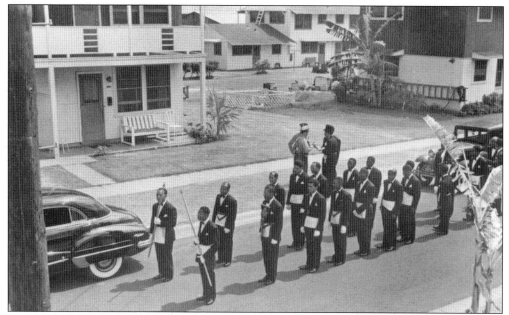

In the Civilian Housing Area III at Pearl Harbor, Masonic Lodge members are shown marching down the street in their segregated community. It did not take long for African Americans to organize mainland-type organizations. Later a chapter of the Order of the Eastern Star, the women's component of Masonry, was founded along with another civic group called Wai Nui Nui. These organizations were the core of the black community. (Courtesy DG.)

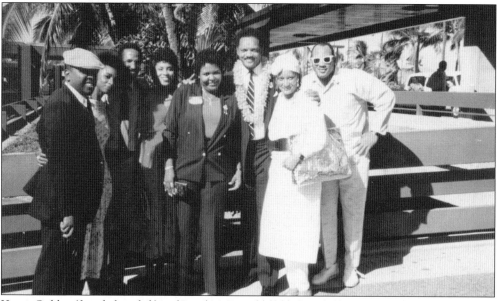

Karen Golden (fourth from left) and Jewel McDonald (fifth from left) are pictured among this group meeting with Jesse Jackson in Honolulu. Jackson and other high-profile blacks were welcomed to the islands by the Honolulu Chapter of the NAACP. Such visits offered local African Americans an opportunity to be kept informed and involved in political issues regarding racism on the mainland. The assassination of Dr. Martin Luther King caused much turmoil at the Schofield Barracks, where hundreds of black soldiers resided. (Courtesy NAACP.)

Rev. Paul Martin came to Hawai'i in the 1940s with the military. After his tour of duty, he chose to reside on O'ahu. Reverend Martin pastored the Pray Center Church of God in Christ in Ewa Beach for many years until his retirement. He is one of a dozen elders who still resides on the island. Their oral histories are being recorded for future generations to enjoy. (Courtesy DG.)

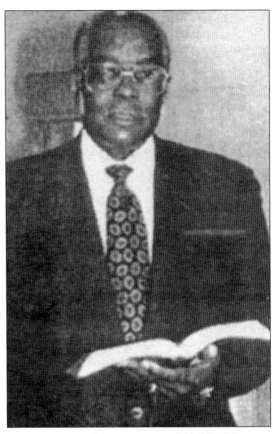

Geynell Lawrence is seated with her friend Craig ? at the Waikiki Yacht Club. The lunch was hosted by the Literary Reading Group. Geynell and Deloris Guttman were responsible for taking on a project that was funded by the Hawai'i State Department of Health to survey people of African descent with HIV/AIDS on the island. Although the sample of participants was small, it was reflective of the larger mainland population. (Courtesy DG.)

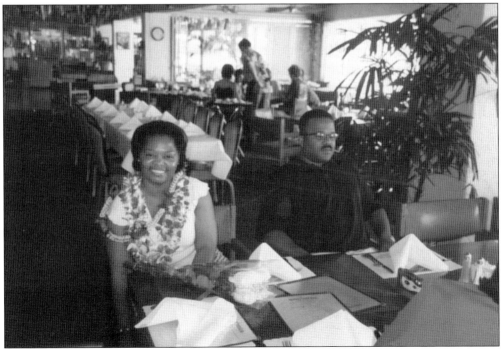

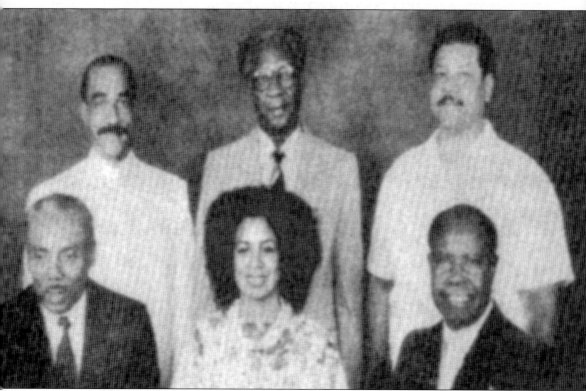

Afro-American Association Hawai'i executive board members are, from left to right, (first row) Orestes Cavness, Regina Gibson-Broome, and Ernest Golden; (second row) Umar Rahsaan, Walter Alexander, and Redmond Humphrey. Golden was a founding member who worked diligently to create an institution for blacks in the islands. Years later, he met a dynamic young lady named Deloris Guttman who shared the same dream for an institution and who founded the African American Diversity Cultural Center Hawai'i. Golden became the vice chairman of the board. (Courtesy EG.)

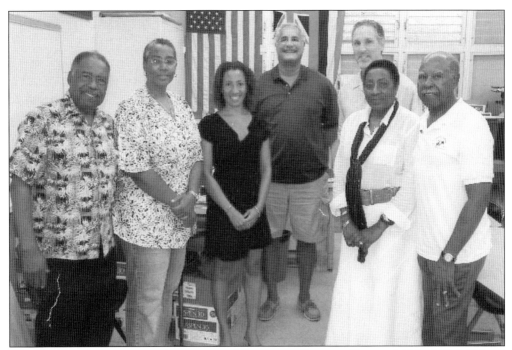

The HIV/AIDS Community Awareness and Prevention Program Team at Mililani High School on O'ahu is sponsored by the African American Diversity Cultural Center Hawai'i. Dr. Arthur Johnson, a physician at Tripler Medical Center, was a keynote speaker. Members of the committee are, from left to right, Bill Malone, Eloise Lewis, Dr. Allison Frances (of Chaminade University), Dr. Arthur Johnson, Russell Motter (history of African American studies teacher at 'Iolani School), Deloris Guttman, and Ernest Golden. (Courtesy DG.)

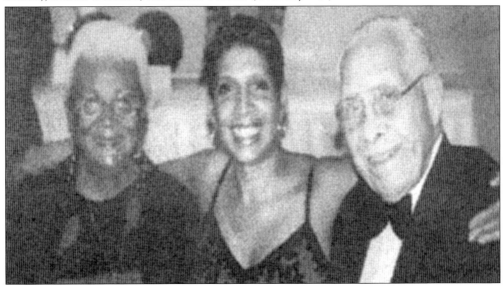

Jeanne Scott (center) poses with her uncle Bob Loving and India Harris. They are friends of the African American Diversity Cultural Center Hawai'i and African Chamber. Scott is a businesswoman who supports every black organization on the island. She is involved with community organizations that promote harmony and ethnic diversity. (Courtesy *Mahogany* magazine.)

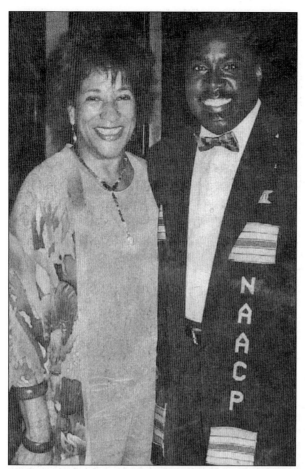

Rea Fox and Alphonso Braggs are pictured here at an NAACP dinner. Braggs is retired from the navy and the president of the local NAACP. This well-known organization has a long history in the islands. It celebrates the birthday of Dr. Martin Luther King and Juneteenth Day, which is the oldest known celebration commemorating the end of slavery in the United States (1865) in Galveston, Texas. (Courtesy *Mahogany* magazine.)

The Alpha Kappa Alpha Sorority Hawai'i is a component of the international organization known by its acronym AKA. Its members are professional women from the military and local residents. (Courtesy Alpha Kappa Alpha Sorority Hawai'i.)

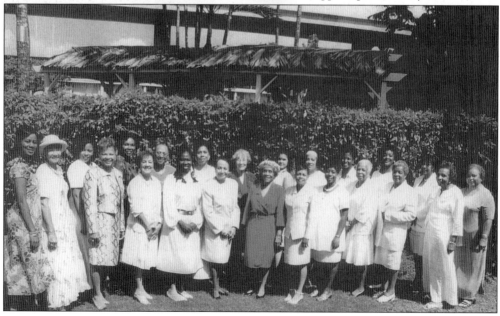

Entrepreneur and community leader Renee Greenwood has lived in Hawai'i for many years. She is a volunteer in the NAACP, has participated in the Dr. Martin Luther King celebration, and collaborates with organizations in an effort to promote civic understanding. (Courtesy *Mahogany* magazine.)

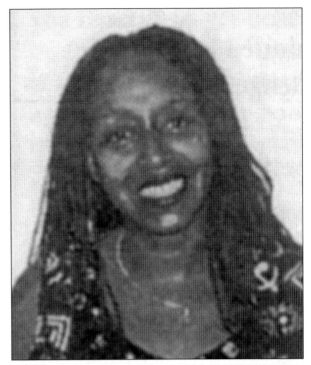

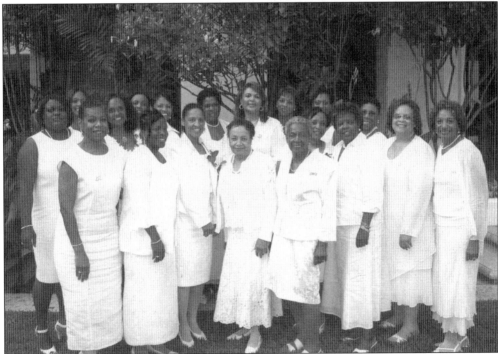

Each year, The Links of Honolulu joins forces with the Honolulu Academy of Arts during Black History Month. This event shares the African diaspora heritage with the people of Hawai'i. Activities are interactive for local children to experience and learn aspects of a culture different from their own. (Courtesy The Links.)

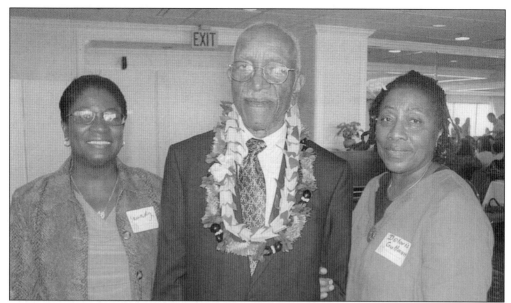

From left to right, Saundy Bratton, Dr. John Hope Franklin, and Deloris Guttman meet for a luncheon at the Plaza Club in Honolulu, where Dr. Franklin shared his experiences with a diverse audience. Dr. Franklin taught at the University of Hawai'i during his early career. This world-renowned historian warmed the hearts and spirits of many island people, including students at the 'Iolani School, where he was a special guest. Dr. John Hope Franklin was the recipient of the first Dan and Maggie Inouye Distinguished Chair in Democratic Ideals at the University of Hawai'i at Manoa. (Courtesy DG.)

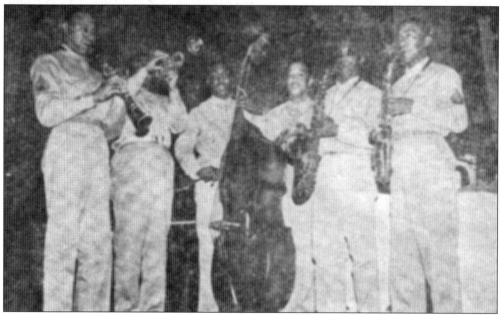

An African American military band plays music at a USO club in Honolulu. During World War II, thousands of black enlisted men were on the island of O'ahu. The USO clubs were responsible for keeping young men entertained while off duty. (Courtesy University of Hawai'i Hamilton Library Archives.)

94

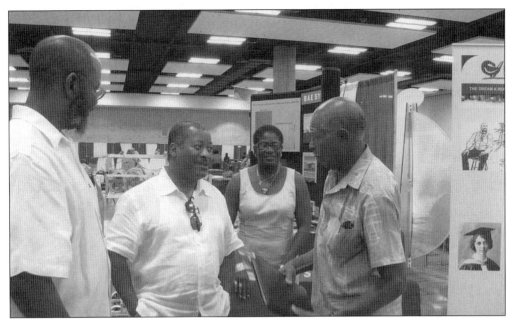

From left to right, Glenn Jolla, Donald King, Saundy Bratton, and Ernest Golden attend the 50th anniversary celebration of the State of Hawai'i at the convention center. The African American Diversity Cultural Center Hawai'i booth was sponsored by DKA Architecture, a Seattle firm that is collaborating with AADCCH and working with the University of Hawai'i School of Architecture. (Courtesy DG.)

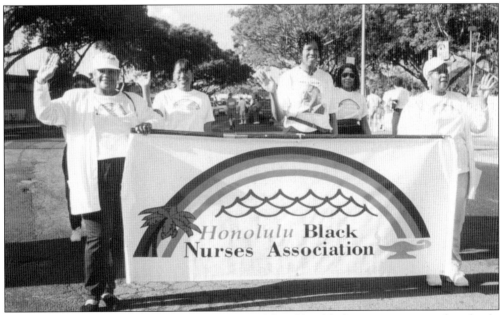

The Honolulu Black Nurses Association is one of the oldest black organizations in the islands. The nurses are representative of all hospitals and private nursing services in Hawai'i. They are involved politically in improving health care for everyone by participating in health fairs and collaborating with community organizations to promote good health agendas. (Courtesy Honolulu Black Nurses.)

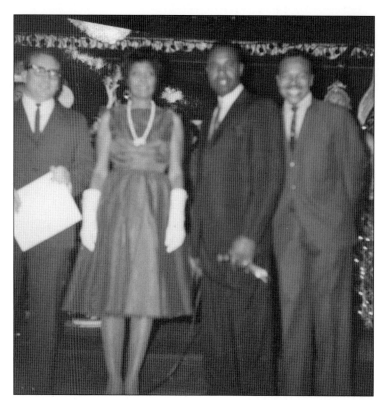

Marva Garrett, who served as the local NAACP president for many years, and Ernest Golden (center) were both active in civic affairs of the community. She lived and worked in the Wai'anae Coast neighborhood. Garrett was involved in the development of the Wai'anae Coast Medical Center to improve the quality of life for Hawaiian people living in that area. (Courtesy NAACP.)

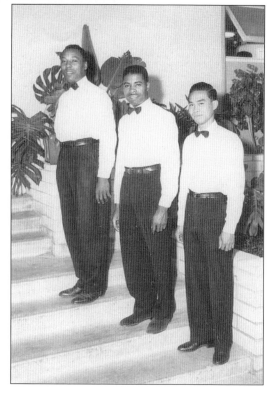

These three African American bellhops were the first in Waikiki. Ernest Golden (center) is one of the young men in this photograph. During World War II, the three most popular hotels were the Royal Hawaiian, the Moana, and the Surf Rider—all in Waikiki. (Courtesy EG.)

Six

FAMILY LIFE OF AFRICAN AMERICANS IN PARADISE

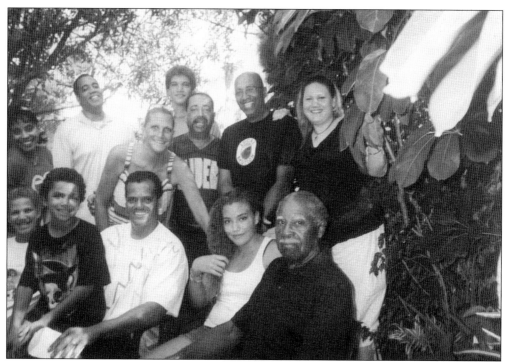

The Golden family is socializing in their Laie backyard on Oʻahu. Their backyard is on the beach, with luscious tropical greenery everywhere. The children were raised in an environment filled with aloha and wide-open space, and the closest neighbor was a mile away during the 1950s. The Koʻolau green sculpted mountains in the background enhanced the family's tropical lifestyle. (Courtesy EG.)

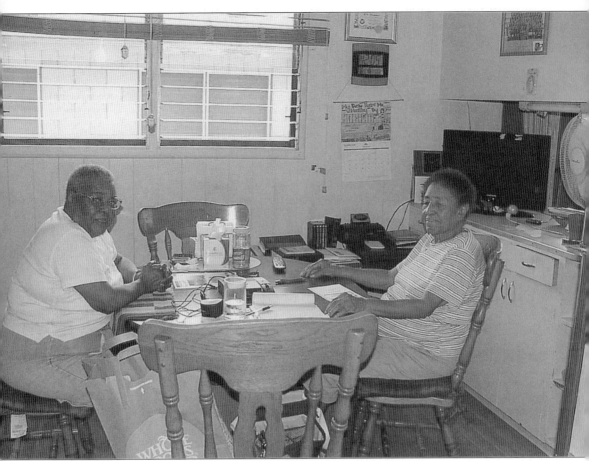

Bertha Dunston (right) poses with her daughter, Bea. Dunston was a civilian worker at Pearl Harbor and lived in the segregated Civilian Housing Area III. Her husband, Nathaniel, came to Hawai'i in 1942. Later they purchased a home in Wai'anae on the leeward side of O'ahu, where Bertha raised her children. Dunston was a member of the Eastern Star and other organizations established by blacks. (Courtesy DG.)

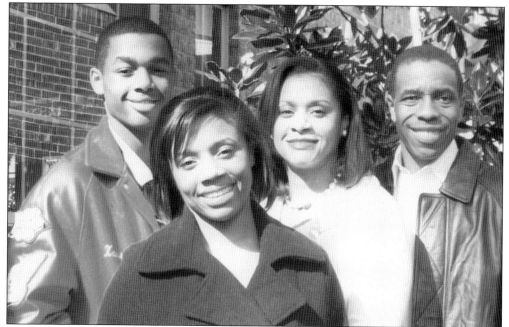

Monica Baisden is with her husband and children in Honolulu. Both the Baisdens are West Point graduates. While living in the islands, Monica became involved with the African Literary Book Group and became editor for the group's newsletter. The Baisdens enjoyed the culture and lifestyle of local people. It was a good learning experience for the family. (Courtesy M. Baisden.)

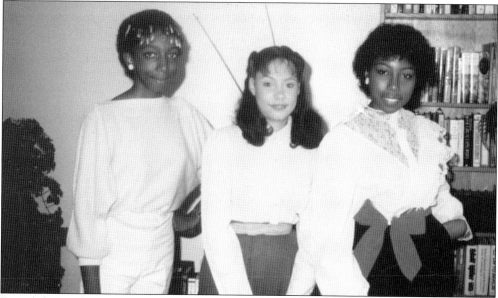

From left to right, Delia Hill, Shelley Hussey, and Gwen Hill are shown in their home in the Makiki neighborhood, where President Obama was raised during the same time period. The Hills and the Obamas were the only black families in the area. Barack Obama was easily identifiable because of his Afro and was often seen around the neighborhood because he attended Punahou School, a block away. During summer sessions, Delia and Gwen took classes at Punahou as well. (Courtesy DG.)

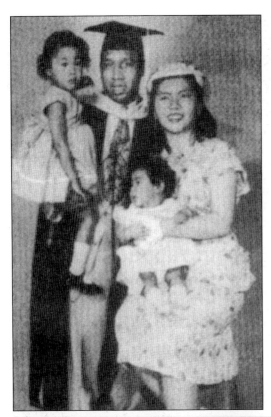

Musician George Wellington poses with his wife, Taeko, and two of their children in Honolulu. Wellington was a noted classical bass player and teacher. He played with the Honolulu Symphony and founded the biennial Hawaii Contrabass Festival. Many of his students went on to become noted musicians around the world. His own sons, daughters, and grandchildren are well-known musicians as well. (Courtesy M. Jackson.)

Gwen Hill (second from left) celebrates her birthday at Farrell's Ice Cream Parlor at Ala Moana Center in Honolulu with a group of unidentified friends. Birthdays are occasions for local children to socialize with their school friends. Farrell's was a great venue for theme parties for children. The hostesses wore outrageous uniforms that children loved. (Courtesy DG.)

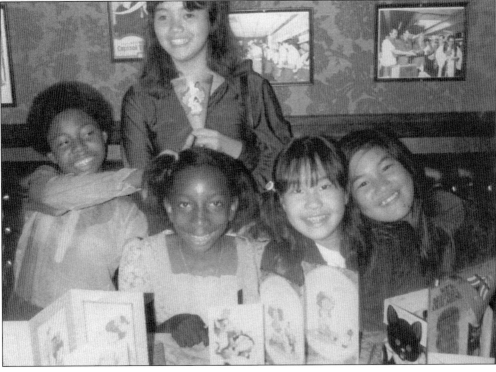

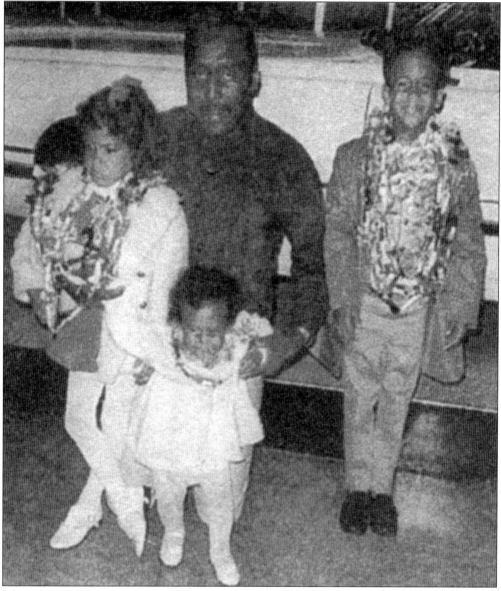

Alonzo DeMello celebrates his birthday with a couple of his children. DeMello's children and grandchildren are ethnically the color of the rainbow. Children are very important in his life, and it makes him smile from ear to ear when he is surrounded by them. (Courtesy A. DeMello.)

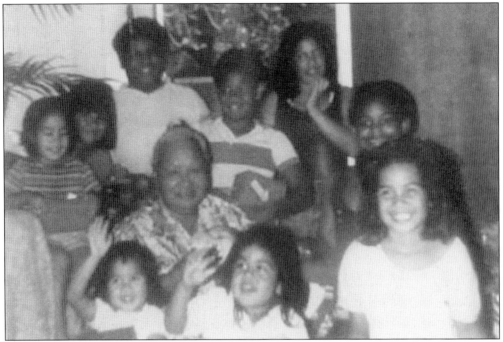

Bridgette Ukaonu's sisters, brothers, and cousins are pictured with their grandmother in Hilo, Hawai'i. Bridgette is part African American and part Hawaiian. Ukaonu's grandparents, Marjorie and William Kailianu, come from an ancestral line of chiefs. Most of her family still lives in Keaukaha on the Big Island. (Courtesy B. Ukaonu.)

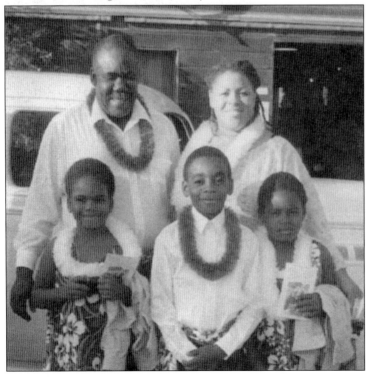

Bridgette Ukaonu poses with her Nigerian husband, Martin, and their three children—from left to right, Chinasa, Chinebu, and Idah. She has never known her African American father. Ukaonu is proud to be part African American and is seeking to find her father or his relatives. Many black men married Hawaiian women and had children. This genealogical history of the Hawaiian people has a rich, collective, cultural heritage. (Courtesy B. Ukaonu.)

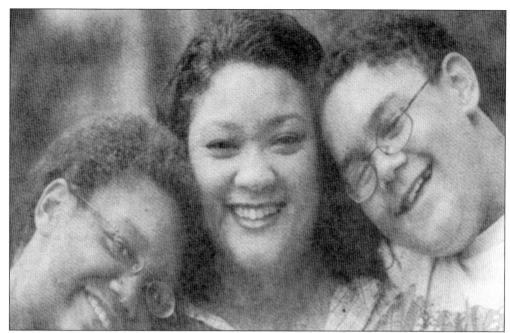

Nanette Miles is with her two children, Brandy and Nicholas Clark. Miles is a single mother raising two children in Honolulu. She is innovative in seeking ways to provide a healthy and safe environment to live. Despite the hardship of raising a family, she is getting a master's degree in speech pathology as a means to improve her economic conditions. (Courtesy *Honolulu Star-Bulletin*.)

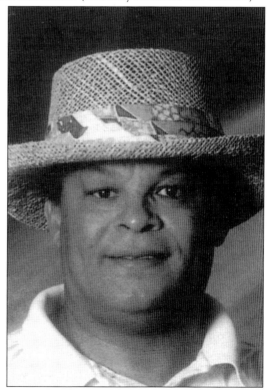

Carrol Cox is an environmentalist who is involved in community conservation work to reduce the impact of environmental justice and racism in the islands. (Courtesy DG.)

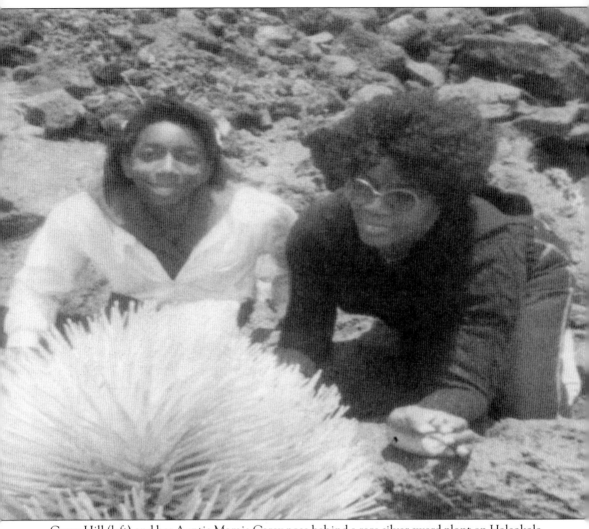

Gwen Hill (left) and her Auntie Mamie Carey pose behind a rare silver sword plant on Haleakala, a mountain on Maui. The beautiful silver sword plants are endangered now due to environmental changes. They grow at specific atmospheric levels on this mountain, and many are very large. (Courtesy DG.)

The Hill family—from left to right, Delia, Deloris, and Gwen—pose for this photograph during Gwen's early years in the Hawaiian Islands. It was rare to see a black mother with children walking down the street, but everyone was friendly and welcomed them. In Waikiki, Japanese tourists would ask to take a picture with the family. They attended the Waikiki Baptist Church several blocks from the beach. (Courtesy DG.)

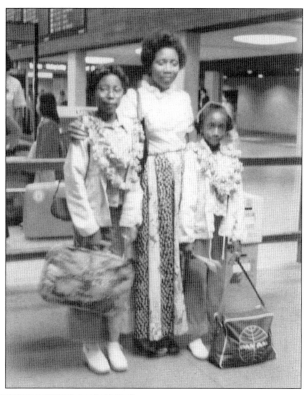

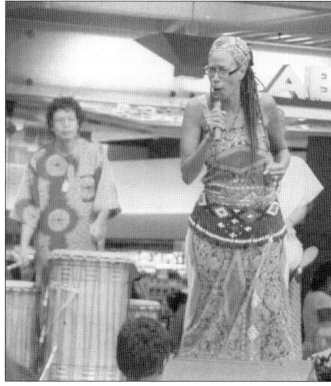

Ashaki Zawadi, a story teller, performs during Cultural Diversity Awareness Day at the Ala Moana Center shopping mall in Honolulu. (Courtesy DG.)

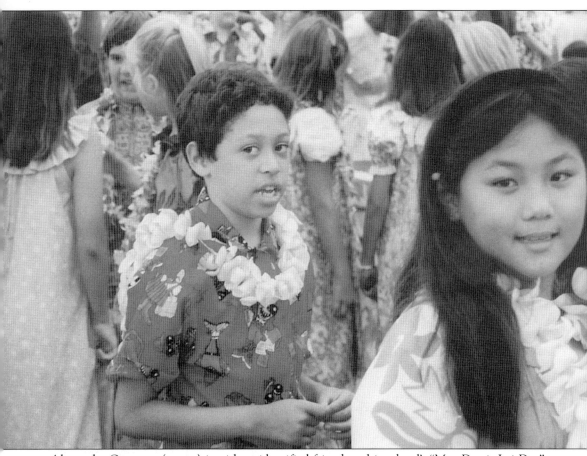

Alexander Guttman (center) is with unidentified friends at his school's "May Day is Lei Day" celebration. It is an annual celebration of Hawaiian culture. The most popular event in schools is the investiture of the Lei Queen and her royal court possession. The royal court ladies are dressed in beautiful rainbow-colored outfits. (Courtesy DG.)

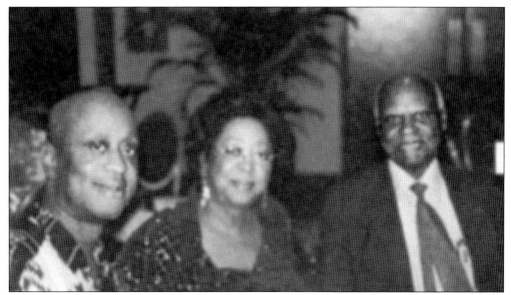

Gregory Harris (left) and his parents, Bettye Jo and Ernest, are at a community event. These occasions are well attended by people of African descent as well as their ethnically diverse friends. (Courtesy *Mahogany* magazine.)

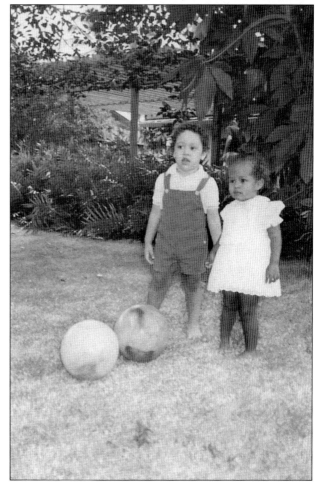

Alexander Guttman and Dakota Langley are playing in the backyard. Children are the conduit to bringing many families together to socialize, especially when they are preschool age. In these environments, many lasting friendships are made. (Courtesy DG.)

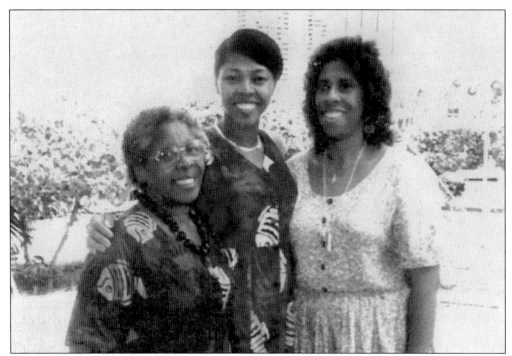

Sandi Sumbry (right) poses with her daughter, Andrea, and her mother, Christine Tucker. Sumbry was a high school special education teacher until her retirement. Andrea and Christine celebrate their birthdays on the same day. Andrea teaches high school in Japan. (Courtesy DG.)

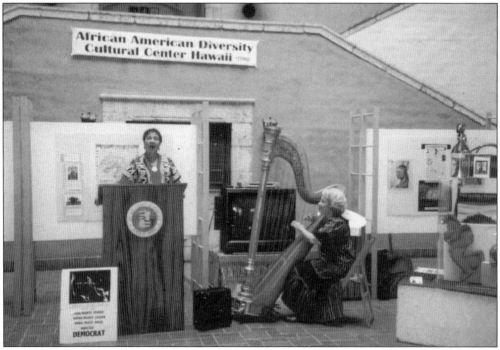

Gwendolyn Johnson (left) and Ruth Freedman (right) appear in a Black History Month concert performance at Honolulu Hale (city hall). (Courtesy DG.)

Seven

BLACK ENTERTAINMENT, SPORTS, AND THEATER IN HAWAI'I

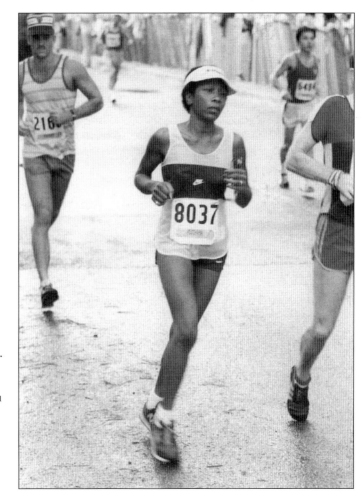

Deloris Hill has run in seven Honolulu marathons. Her best time was 3 hours, 38 minutes. She began her training with the Honolulu Marathon Association. The training was a gradual running regiment each week that continued until she reached the 25-mile duration. (Courtesy DG.)

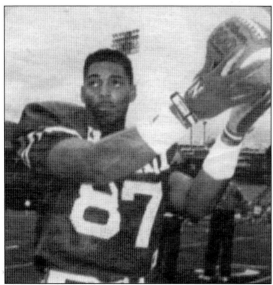

Darrick Branch was a University of Hawai'i football player. During his senior season, Branch put Hawai'i football on the map nationally, as he helped the university to achieve its first Western Athletic Conference championship. His career spanned the globe from the CFL to NFL to Europe. (Courtesy *Honolulu Star-Bulletin*.)

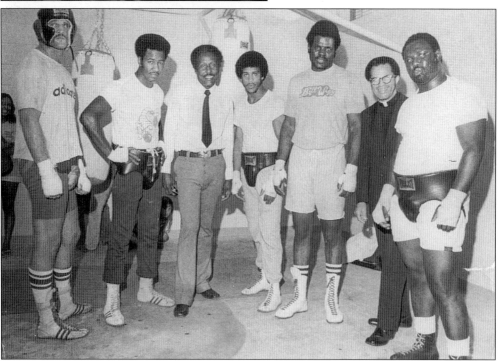

Alonzo DeMello has always been involved in boxing and working with the youth. He organized the DeMello Boxing Club in Honolulu. During World War II, boxing and baseball were the two largest sports activities in the Islands. At some boxing matches at Schofield Barracks, more than 10,000 people were in attendance. Boxing became legal during the territorial era until statehood and was under joint military and civilian administration. The Hawaiian word for boxing is *mokomoko*. In January 1913, the War Department transferred the 25th Infantry Regiment, a black company, to Fort Shafter. There were four boxers in the regiment—Hollie Giles, a welterweight of 155 pounds; Morgan, a heavyweight at 190 pounds; Carson, a light heavyweight; and Ananias Harris, another light heavyweight. (Courtesy A. DeMello.)

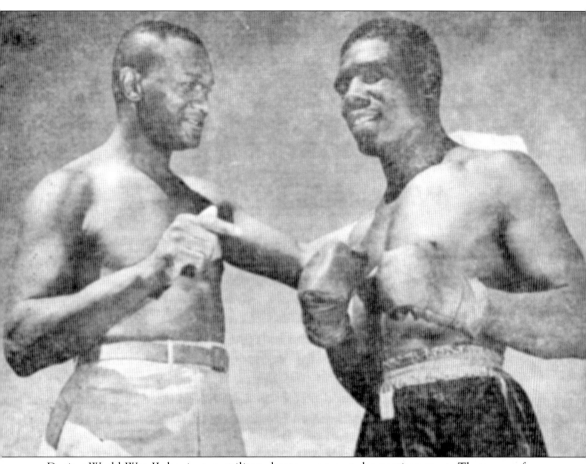

During World War II, boxing on military bases was a popular pastime sport. There were four outstanding African American boxers in the islands: Ted King, Howard E. Dorsey, Eugene Hicks, and Nathaniel Pratt. They had an impressive record of knockouts. (Courtesy *New Pacific* magazine.)

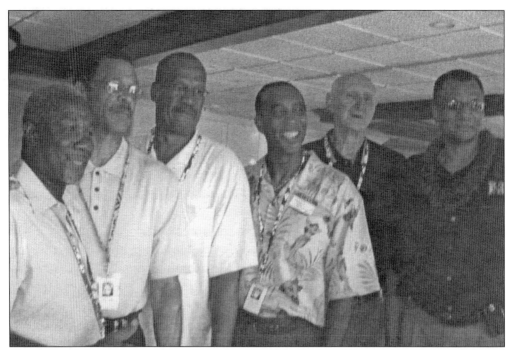

Shown from left to right are Jerome Freeman, John Penebacker, Al Davis, Dwight Holiday, head coach Red Rocha, and Bob Nash. These basketball teammates were known as the "Fabulous Five" and were the most popular players at the University of Hawai'i. (Courtesy *Honolulu Star-Bulletin*.)

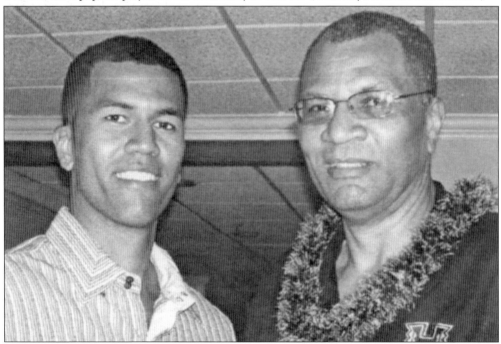

Bob Nash is with his son, Bobby. Nash was an assistant basketball coach at the University of Hawai'i for many years before becoming the head coach for the University of Hawai'i basketball team. (Courtesy *Mahogany* magazine.)

112

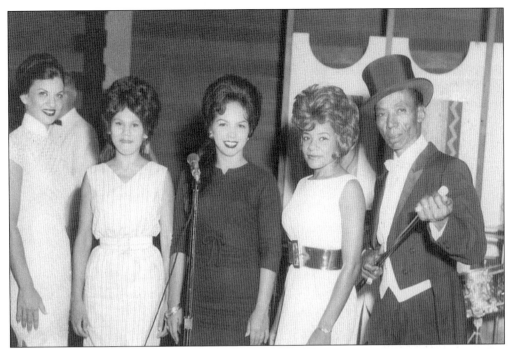

Hampton Brazell (right), Audrey McClellan (second from right), and their unidentified friends were entertainers at a nightclub in Honolulu during the 1940s. Brazell was a businessman with multiple talents. During that era, black people had to be creative in generating wholesome entertainment. (Courtesy PS.)

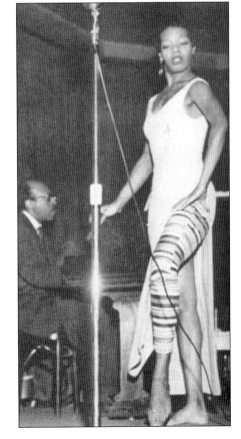

Maya Angelou's brother, Bailey, brought his grief-stricken sister to Hawai'i, where he had found a singing gig for her in a Waikiki nightclub after she returned from Ghana to California to help with the civil rights movement and planned to work for Malcolm X. After her plane landed in California, she learned that Malcolm X had been assassinated. (Courtesy K. Takara.)

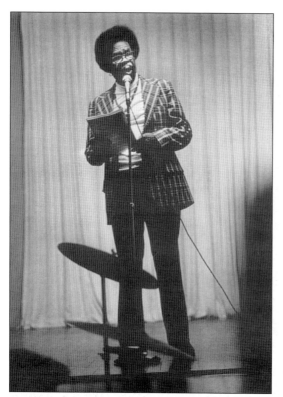

Frank Marshall Davis read his poetry at the University of Hawai'i and Howard University in 1970s. Davis was a forerunner in the literary history of African Americans. At age 17, he found his niche for writing poetry in college. One his best collections is *47th Street: Poems*. (Courtesy K. Takara.)

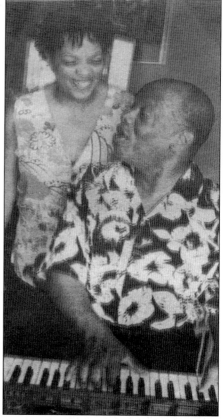

Azure McCall and Tennyson Stephens are entertaining at a venue in Honolulu. The McCall and Stephens duo have been performing together for three decades at Honolulu nightclubs and community events. (Courtesy *Honolulu Star-Bulletin*.)

Bobby Thursby, blues singer, performed in Waikiki clubs for many years. He is known for singing down-home, hole-in-the-wall blues the old fashioned way. (Courtesy *Mahogany* magazine.)

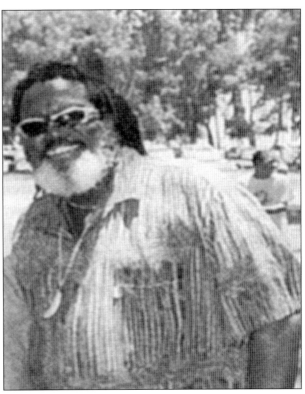

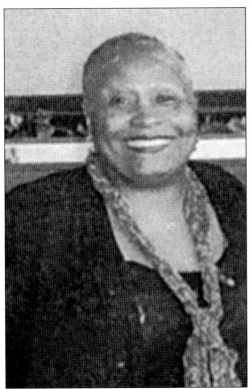

Micki Fine is a performer and comedian who dramatizes plantation-style spirituals and tells humorous jokes about Southern lifestyles. (Courtesy Trinity Baptist Church.)

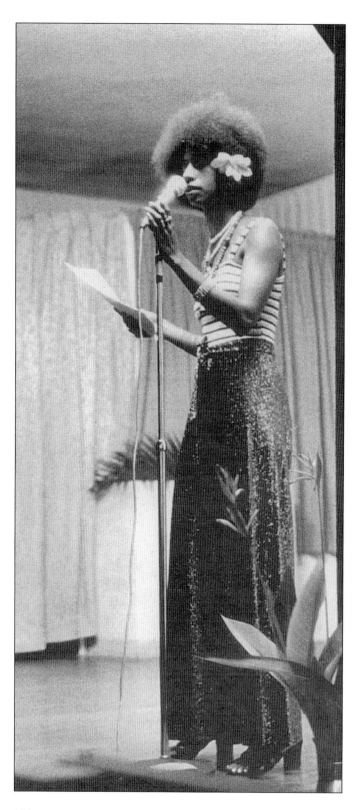

Kathryn Waddell Takara reads her poetry at a gathering in Honolulu. Takara has worked in China and Africa. Her passion for decades has been writing poetry, performing, and collaborating with well-known people like Ishmael Reed. (Courtesy K. Takara.)

James "Trummy" Young was one of the world's greatest trombonists. Young played with Louis Armstrong and Duke Ellington's big bands around the world. He performed for many years in the Garden Bar at the Hawaiian Village with jazz singer Ethel Azama and the John Norris Dixieland band at Trappers in the Hyatt Regency Waikiki. (Courtesy *Honolulu Star-Bulletin*.)

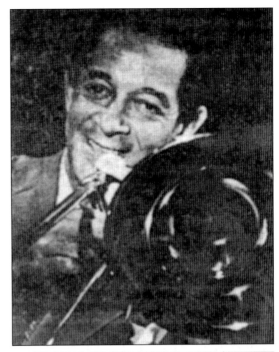

Adela Chu is an internationally known dancer, choreographer, musician, and arts instructor from Panama. She is a founder of the Honolulu First Night's samba parade and the Afro-Jazz Dancers. Over the past 20 years, she has choreographed and performed all over the Hawaiian Islands, Brazil, Mexico, Jamaica, Holland, and United States. (Courtesy *Mahogany* magazine.)

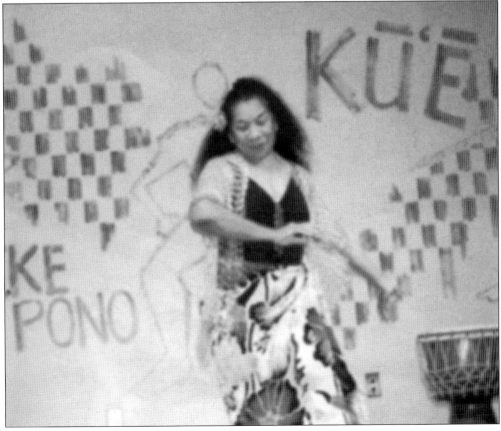

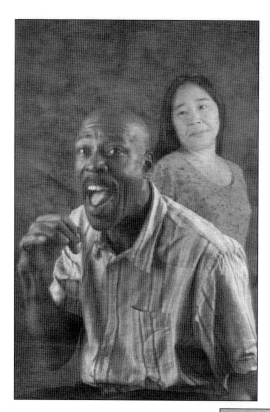

Jim Andres and Jodie Yamada are husband and wife in the play *Yohen* that focuses on the couple's marriage. Yamada is a Japanese war bride, and Andres was a boxer with Olympic potential. They met in Japan. The word *yohen* is a Japanese term for an unintentional flaw created while firing a piece of pottery. (Courtesy *Honolulu Star-Bulletin*.)

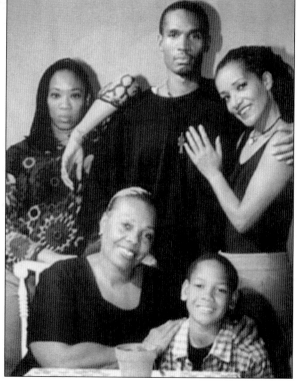

The cast of *A Raisin in the Sun* includes, from left to right, (first row) Della Graham and Ronson Spells; (second row) Lillian Jones, Trevor Graham, and Annette Kauahikaua. This was the first time an August Wilson play was performed in Honolulu, and it received rave reviews and a sellout every night it played. (Courtesy Honolulu *Star-Bulletin*.)

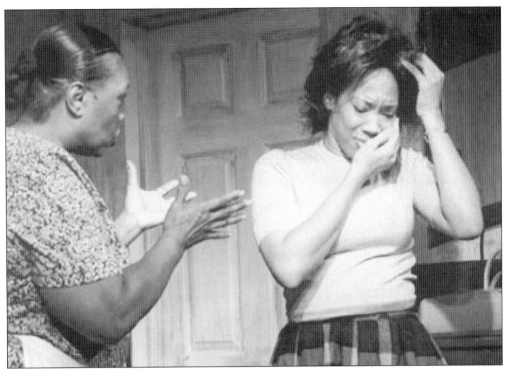

Della Graham (left) and Lillian Jones appear in a scene from *A Raisin in the Sun*. The story line is potent and remains timely. (Courtesy *Honolulu Star-Bulletin*.)

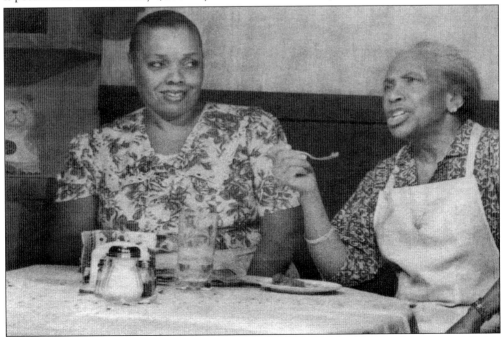

Della Graham (left) and Judith Henry act in another scene. Henry plays Mrs. Johnson in *A Raisin in the Sun*. Her role as the neighbor is a very important part in the story. (Courtesy *Honolulu Star-Bulletin*.)

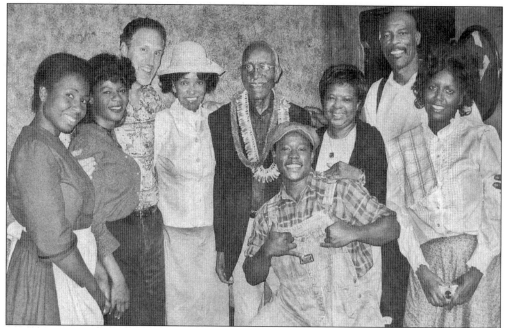

The cast of *Joe Turner's Come and Gone* appears with historian Dr. John Hope Franklin (center). They are, from left to right, Jeanne Herring, Deborah Young, Russell Motter, Annette Kauahikaua, Franklin, Svada Gilmore, Sandra Simms, Jim Andrews, and Deneen Thompson. The Actors Group sponsored a series of August Wilson plays at the Yellow Brick Studio in Honolulu. (Courtesy *Honolulu Star-Bulletin*.)

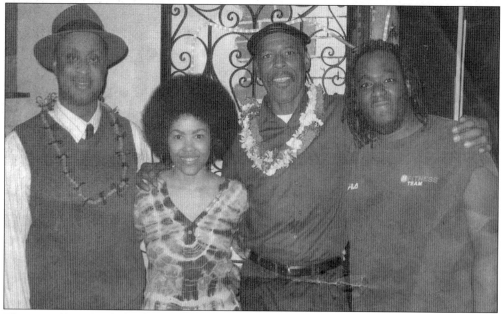

The cast of *Jitney* includes, from left to right, Gregory Harris, Kesha Diodato, Jim Andrews, and Derrick Brown. This play is about relationships that are personal and intergenerational and shape the foundations of our lives. *Jitney* evolved out of the turbulent 1960s and still resonates today. (Courtesy *Honolulu Advertiser*.)

In this scene from *Jitney* are, from left to right, (first row) Gregory Harris and Billy Hall; (second row) Kesha Diodato, Christopher Smith, and Jim Andrews. This play identifies the intergenerational relationships that are the foundation of the African American lives which evolved out of the turbulent 1960s and still resonate in black communities today. (Courtesy *Honolulu Advertiser*.)

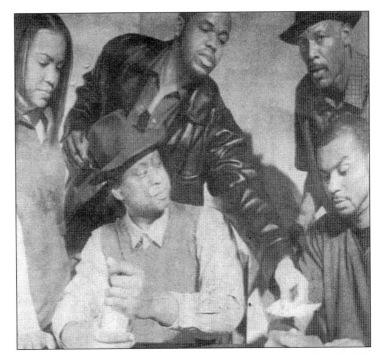

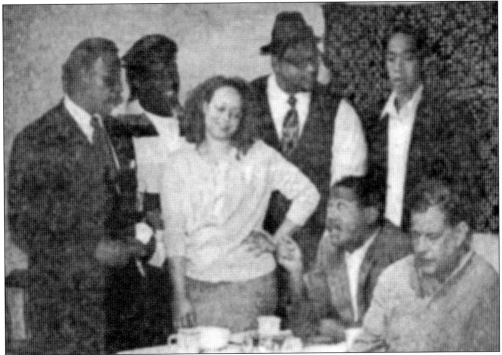

The cast of *Two Trains Running* includes, from left to right, (standing) Honey Brown, Derrick Brown, Donna Sallee, Gemini Burke, and Moses Goode; (seated) Leonard Piggee and Russell Goode. This August Wilson play is about an inner-city neighborhood in Pittsburgh, Pennsylvania. One focus is a prisoner, another is chasing easy money, and the third is facing the loss of his business due to urban development. (Courtesy *Honolulu Star-Bulletin*.)

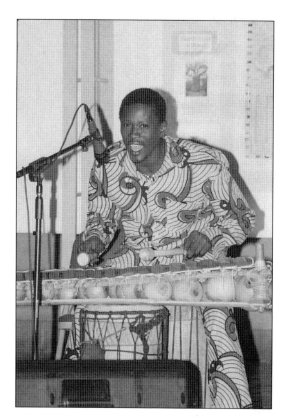

Seku Camara sings and plays an African xylophone at Honolulu Hale during the Black History Exhibition opening ceremony. Camara is from Africa and lives in Honolulu. He is an accomplished African musician. (Courtesy DG.)

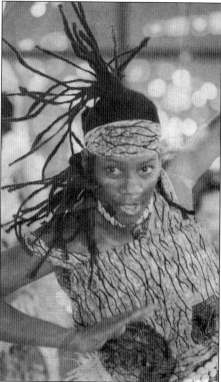

African dancer Atijah Porch performs at schools and community events. She performed siente, a dance from Guinea, West Africa, at the Ethnic Heritage Activities Day at Kapi'olani Community College in Honolulu. (Courtesy *Honolulu Advertiser.*)

Moussa Bangoura sings and plays an African instrument at Honolulu Hale during the Black History Exhibition opening ceremony. He is an African percussionist who ignites the spirit of the ancestors and then communes with them. (Courtesy DG.)

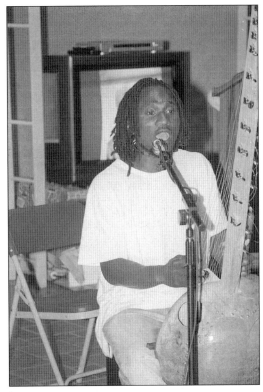

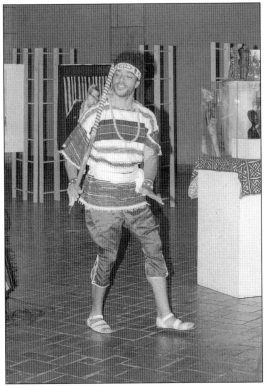

Thomas Young is performing an Ethiopian dance at Honolulu Hale during the Black History Exhibition ceremony. His performances touched the inner soul's consciousness and brought it to the surface for those in tune with spirituality to enjoy and appreciate. (Courtesy DG.)

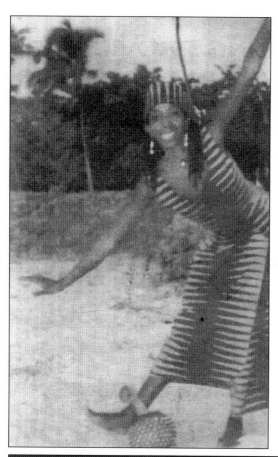

Gwen Hill, an African dancer, studied under the tutelage of African griots in Ghana for three to four months annually for many years. The elders initiated her into their tribal ceremonies and gave her an African name, Adoulaye. (Courtesy DG.)

Ruby Shang and Earnest Morgan of Dance Hawai'i are shown here performing. Morgan was born and raised in Hawai'i, and his essence was intertwined with the presence of the elements—fire, earth, water, and air. This dance pays homage to Pele, the Hawaiian goddess. (Courtesy of Dance Hawai'i.)

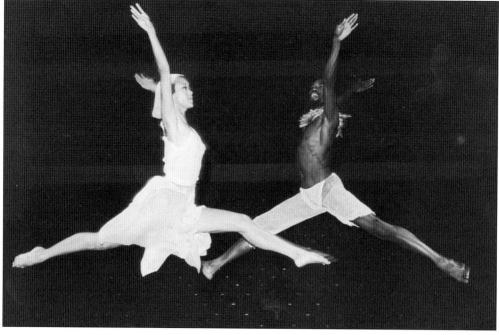

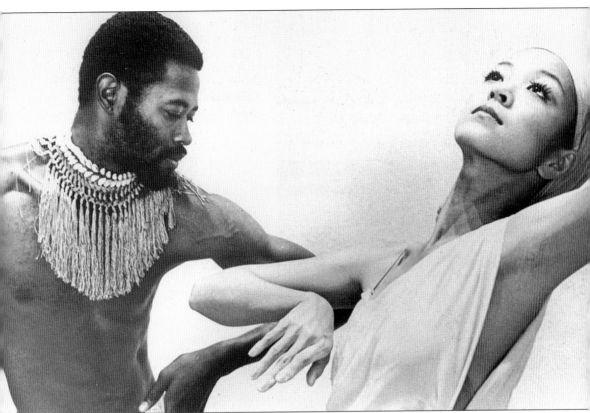

Earnest Morgan and Ruby Shang perform a dance piece called "Halape," inspired by an earthquake on the Big Island of Hawai'i. This dance is rooted in the soul or being of the dancers and symbolizes the volcano that is the deity of Pele, which embraces the vitality of nature and human beings. (Courtesy Dance Hawai'i.)

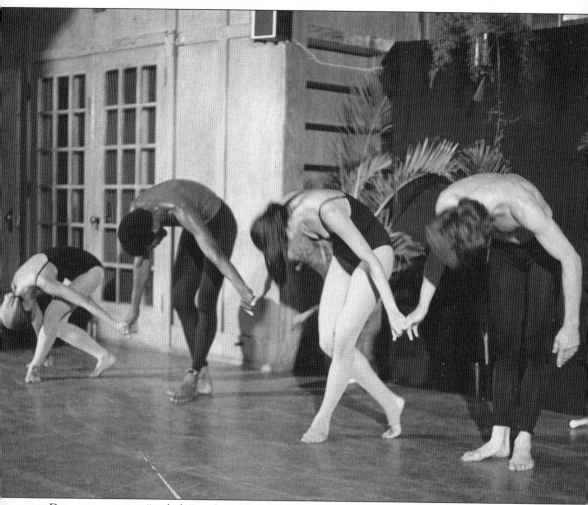

Dancers are saying "mahalo" to the audience by bowing at the end of a performance in Honolulu. Dance Hawai'i focuses its pieces on the ancient Hawaiian culture. Its stories are provocative and enriching for audiences. (Courtesy Dance Hawai'i.)

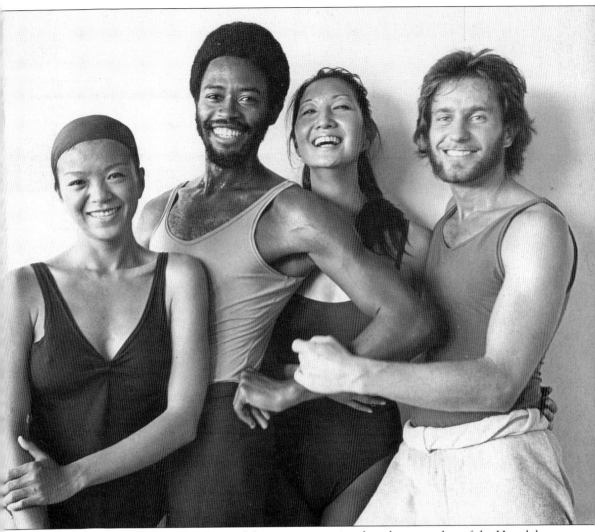

Earnest Morgan, a choreographer and dancer, was appointed as choreographer of the Honolulu City Ballet Company by the late mayor Frank Fasi. The troupe's performances added an intellectual atmosphere to island lifestyle, similar to those seen at the San Francisco and New York Performing Arts Centers. Morgan later founded the Dance Hawai'i troupe. Shown here, from left to right, are Ruby Shang, Morgan, Trina Nahm-Mijo, and Richard Koob. (Courtesy Dance Hawai'i.)

www.arcadiapublishing.com

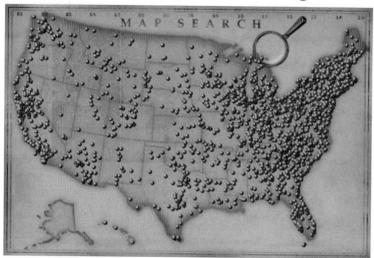

Discover books about the town where you grew up, the cities where your friends and families live, the town where your parents met, or even that retirement spot you've been dreaming about. Our Web site provides history lovers with exclusive deals, advanced notification about new titles, e-mail alerts of author events, and much more.

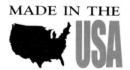

Find Your Place in History.